WOMEN AND COMMUNICATIVE POWER:
THEORY, RESEARCH, AND PRACTICE

* * * * * * * * * * * * *

A monograph developed from the
Speech Communication Association Seminar Series
Denver, Colorado

* * * * * * * * * * * *

CAROL ANN VALENTINE, Ph.D.
Arizona State University

NANCY HOAR, Ed.D.
Western New England College

Published by the Speech Communication Association
5105 Backlick Road, Bldg. E
Annandale, Virginia 22003

Library of Congress Catalog Card No. 88-63211

ISBN 0-944811-01-9

TABLE OF CONTENTS

This monograph, "Women and Communicative Power: Theory, Research and Practice" takes a contemporary concern and explores the links among women and communicative power from a variety of perspectives. Theory, research and practice are brought together in a format that explores, then synthesizes.

Here, scholars in communication analyze the issues and point directions for future research. The transitional sections are the connective tissue that summarize the main points of the previous work and tie into the subsequent section.

Implicitly we believe we have broken new ground in both content and method. These scholars are committed both to the study of communicative power and to how increasing knowledge of communicative power will enable women to use their already honed communication skills to even greater advantage.

Now comes the challenge for all of us readers, scholars, and reader/scholars. All knowledge begins with fitful and challenging starts. There is no doubt here. We will each find assignments in this collection and each effort will advance the knowledge of the connective tissue between the variables of communication and power.

The topic and format make this monograph an ideal reader for a gender communication course and enhance its power as a text supplement. Since questions of communicative power are central in such courses this monograph promises to contribute considerable insight and raise provocative questions while breaking new ground in the area of women and communication.

Nancy and I are indebted to Nancy Henley for the concept of this monograph, to Keith M. Campbell for the reality of the monograph and to each of the scholars contributing thoughts, efforts, and directions for the future study of women and communicative power.

Carol Ann Valentine

WOMEN AND COMMUNICATIVE POWER:
INTRODUCTION

Generally people write about books that changed their lives. This seminar was conceived, less universally, from a book's subtitle. *Body Politics: Power, Sex, and Nonverbal Communication* by Nancy Henley might not have changed my life but the subtitle "Power, Sex, and Non-verbal Communication" certainly jolted my perceptions.

How could I be so naive? One of those waves of "Why didn't you ever think about these connections before?" washed over me. Those with the *power* to define appropriate *communication* are in many cases *men*. What an obvious connection.

In my college career the formal study of power followed reading Richard Neustadt's *Presidential Power*. The essence of the book was that power is influence. I suppose one could argue that influence does not necessarily equal control, but some connection is inescapable. Actually I suspect it was "set up." I was primed after reading *Women and Men Speaking* by Cheris Kramarae and Carol Gilligan's *In a Different Voice*. As women, we live in a male-dominated society and these people have power over us in many ways. Naively, I had not thought directly about how men achieve and maintain power through communication.

Many of those with the power to shape our reality are men. In the academic world, the presidents, deans, and chairs are likely to be male. These people can control our tenure and esteem. Is it too strong to say that for many of us our economic, psychological and sociological realities are controlled by men? I'm sure there are readers who respond "It's not true." In those cases, the statement is likely to be partially true. Again, this seminar addressed degrees of communicative power.

Whatever the percentage of male power in one's life, this seminar sought to address this and related topics. What are the connections between power, communication, and gender? How significant are the links?

With this question, the SCA 1985 seminar on "Women and Communicative Power" was proposed to offer a forum for discussion of connections among these three variables. The reader will likely agree that the goal was met. The papers

Carol Valentine is an Associate Professor of Communication and Women's Studies, Arizona State University, Tempe, AZ 85287-1205.

that follow are an exciting expansion of academic variables of power, gender, and communication.

Nancy Hoar begins our examination with a clear statement about power. Power is related to manners and politeness.

Frances Sayers explores powerful and powerless speech and suggests means for making communication more effective. Assessment of the situations is seen as critical and Sayers stresses that neither powerful nor powerless speech is effective in every situation. The critical need for flexibility in speech behavior is stressed. Sayers also raises interesting methodological questions . . . . . and answers them.

Constance Staley crystalizes the dilemmas of power and influence that women managers face. Why do women managers face doubts about their communicative power? Be sure to read this one, too.

Banisa Saint Damian is a sociologist who looks at communication from a societal influence point of view. Together we look at cross-cultural influences on women's vocal communicative power.

Barbara Crawford draws ten conclusions about "women and their communicative power" based on a review of her personal professional experience. These are powerful.

Suzanne Condray moves in still another direction. Her perspective is media-oriented. The National Organization for Women has been influential and therefore wielded power. As a result, NOW's strategies are of interest to all.

Valerie Endress takes the concept of women's relation to communication to another realm. Endress states it clearly and without equivocation. Women's communication is generally devalued. Particularly in a public speaking context, Endress argues we present and value male models. It is time to stop this.

Beverly Romberger steps back into time and place to draw a similar point. Women are taught that men have the communicative power. The oral histories of Pennsylvania women simply state the point from another and very interesting perspective.

Carol Spitzak makes a nifty point. We must go beyond content of women's language if we are to understand power connections. Power has its communicative dimension but it also has logical underpinnings. These too need exploration.

Nancy Hoar, a participant and critic, concludes with a synthesis and evaluation of the papers. This essay goes well beyond "further research is needed." The reader will leave the seminar summary with a clear sense of some issues central to the connections between women and communicative power and will begin an exciting research agenda.

Now we embark upon our exploration of women, men, power and communication. Hoar explores the relationship of gender, status, politeness, and power. Hoar's conclusion is a promising and powerful one. "By changing her communicative behavior, a women can influence the way others respond to her and she can begin to be the architect of her place in society."

Nancy Hoar

GENDERLECT, POWERLECT, AND POLITENESS

Genderlect is speech that contains features that mark it as stereotypically masculine or feminine. To be sure, genderlect does imply more intrasex homogeniety than actually exists (Kramerae, 1981, p. 92; Thorne, Kramerae & Henley, 1983, p.14); even so, the term **genderlect** is a useful label to refer to the set of features that mark stereotypical masculine and feminine speech. Moreover, the term **genderlect** is useful in referring to **expected** as well as observed behavior because "we know more about which gender-based message cues people are expected to use than about how often a given individual actually uses any of these cues in a given setting" (Bate, 1988, p. 56); and expectations and stereotypes are, of course, powerful filters in our perceptions of others. The term **genderlect** need not be limited to speech, however; it can be extended to include nonverbal communication that is stereotypically masculine or feminine.[1]

Although genderlect may seem to be a basic communication descriptor, it is actually a derived descriptor, for it is dependent upon **powerlect**, i.e., communication that contains features that indicate the relative status of its users. Genderlect is actually the expression of powerlect interpreted according to culturally based gender expectations. We will examine the work of several communication scholars to see why this is so. We will also see why gender and power are concomitant with a third factor -- politeness.

GENDERLECT AND POWERLECT

The influence of gender upon communication has intrigued linguists for the past two decades. Robin Lakoff's "Language and Woman's Place" (1973) was a spark that stimulated investigations by many other researchers. Lakoff's description, a product of observation and introspection, focused on the syntactic and lexical features that characterize feminine genderlect. The most salient features are questions in place of statements and requests, tag questions, "weak" expletives, and "fluffy" adjectives of approval or disapproval.

Questions, of course, have a rightful place in discourse; their primary purpose is to obtain information which the asker does not know or is uncertain of. When questions take the place of statements, however, the speaker seems tentative

Nancy Hoar is an Associate Professor in the Department of English and Humanities at Western New England College, Springfield, MA 01119.

and unwilling to make an assertion of fact or opinion. Compare a) and b) as responses to the question, "Where do you want to go tonight?"

a) To dinner and then to a film.
b) To dinner and then to a film?

The second response is weaker. This weakness and tentativeness is also seen in the speaker who uses a question to make a request. Again compare a) and b):

a) Check under the hood.
b) Do you think you could check under the hood?

Lakoff contended that the person who uses b) can more easily be refused than can the person who uses a). Lakoff also stated that these weaker forms, the b) forms, are more likely to appear in the speech of women than of men.

An interesting type of question is the tag question; i.e., a question that immediately follows a statement and that questions the statement: "That's your car, isn't it?" Lakoff explained that the tag question "...isn't it?" (with rising, not level or falling, intonation) communicates a degree of uncertainty intermediate between that expressed by a yes-no question ("Is that your car?") and that expressed by a statement ("That's your car"). Often, however, the asker of tag questions is looking for confirmation when it isn't necessary (That was a funny film, wasn't it?"). As a result, the asker seems to lack conviction and confidence and to have no ideas of his/her own.

Lakoff differentiated between "weak" expletives and "strong" expletives. She contended that weak expletives, such as "oh dear," "golly," and "darn," are more likely to be found in the speech of women than in the speech of men. Men are more likely to use strong expletives such as "shit" or "damn." Lakoff asserted that weak expletives convey docility and less emotional involvement, while strong expletives convey strength and involvement. Weak expletives are suitable for unimportant topics:

"Oh darn, the lettuce is gritty."

but not for more important topics:

"Oh darn, they murdered the manager."

Conversely, strong expletives are suitable for strong topics:

"Oh Christ, they murdered the manager."

but not for less important topics:

"Oh Christ, the lettuce is gritty.

People who take strong stands on important topics are considered stronger than people who exclaim over less important topics. Lakoff suggested that because the use of strong expletives is socially less acceptable for women, women are precluded from an equal opportunity to assert themselves in a credible manner.

Finally, Lakoff noted that "fluffy" adjectives of approval or disapproval are more likely to be found in women's speech than in the speech of men. Among such adjectives are "divine," "adorable," and "sweet." These fluffy adjectives are usually applied to trivial topics such as clothing and kittens but not to serious topics. Serious, "real world" topics are more likely to be described with "neutral" adjectives such as "great" or "terrific." Compare a) and b):

> a) "What a great ad campaign."
> b) "What a divine ad campaign."

Speakers who use fluffy adjectives convey triviality and a lack of importance. No woman manager who is serious about her career would exclaim b).

Lakoff's descriptions have been examined and re-examined by other scholars. Some studies have confirmed Lakoff's work (Bailey & Timm, 1976; Hartman, 1976, 1978), while others have not (Dubois & Crouch, 1975; Kuykendall, 1980; Metts & Bryan, 1984; Valian, 1977). Perhaps this lack of consistent confirmation or disconformation is due to situational variables that have not remained constant in these and other investigations (Brown, 1976; Brown & Levinson, 1980; Crosby & Nyquist, 1977; O'Barr, 1982).

Linguists are not the only scholars who are interested in genderlect. Other communication scholars such as Cheris Kramerae have found additional lexical and semantic features of feminine language, particularly stereotypical feminine language (i.e. feminine genderlect). Kramerae studied stereotypes of feminine language by examining the captions of cartoons appearing in the *New Yorker* (1974). The most salient features of feminine genderlect she identified were "trivial" topics, apologies and self-deprecation, and hedges and vague qualifiers. She also found examples of the fluffy adjectives and "toned-down" swearing described by Lakoff.

Kramerae found that unlike men, who talked about influential topics like business and politics, women often talked about food, drink, life style, and the care of one's spouse and children, topics that are rarely found in headlines. If we assume that people's talk is a reflection of their thoughts, then women, stereotypically, are more interested in "trivia" than in "newsworthy" topics. A person who prefers the trivial to the newsworthy is not considered to be a decisive or influential person.

Kramerae also found that female characters were more likely to blame themselves and engage in apologies and self- deprecation, whereas men were more likely to place blame and deprecation elsewhere. For example, in one cartoon a husband and wife are watching television news and the wife exclaims, "I keep forgetting. Which is the good guy, Prince Souvanna Phouma or Prince Souphanouvong?" The woman blames her confusion upon her own memory. Kramerae suggested that if the speaker had been the husband, the caption would more likely have been "Damn it! How are we supposed to remember which one is Souvanna Phouma and which one is Souvanouvong!" He would be placing the blame on the similarity of the two foreign names.

The female characters in the *New Yorker* cartoon captions also used hedges and vague qualifiers such as "sort of" and "kind of." Compare a) and b):

> a) We've seen this before.
> b) We've sort of seen this before.

Hedged statements like b) make the speaker seem unsure and unassertive. The hedged statement is less forceful.

Even though Kramerae's data reflect stereotypes of women's speech rather than speech women actually use, and even though this data is more than a decade old, these stereotypes are far from inactive. Every semester since 1982 I have constructed captions containing these features of feminine genderlect, as well as captions containing features of masculine genderlect and captions with "neutral" speech; and I have asked my undergraduate students to visualize the cartoon which might accompany these captions and to identify the speaker of the caption. Every semester my students identify masculine genderlect speakers as male and feminine genderlect speakers as female (or as "wimpy" males).

In addition to Lakoff's anecdotal study and Kramerae's study of stereotypical speech, there are other methods of studying gender-influenced communication. Candace West and Donald Zimmerman collected covertly recorded conversations between male-female dyads in a nonexperimental environment and analyzed them, using Harvey Sachs rules governing the organization of conversations, namely that one person is suppposed to speak at a time (1975, 1979, 1983). West and Zimmerman found that women followed these rules but men did not: the men began before the women had finished speaking and the women were forced to surrender (though not without protest) their conversational turns (also, see Spender, 1980). Also, women not only had their "conversational space" violated but they often paused longer before beginning to speak after men had finished their turns, thus avoiding encroaching upon men's "conversational space."

In addition, West and Zimmerman found that women had less control over the length and viability of their discourse, and less control over the topics of discourse. When men introduced ideas, women usually accepted and pursued these ideas. However, when women introduced ideas, men often ignored the women's ideas and pursued their own interests. In one segment of conversation a woman asked her male partner about his term paper and listened politely to his response. She then tried unsuccessfully four times to talk about her own term paper, and each time she was interrupted by his request for a cigarette or a match. Clearly the leadership she may have shown in initiating the topic soon evaporated.

Perhaps even more disheartening than being interrupted or circumvented is being ignored. This, too, happened to women but not to men. In the conversations recorded by Pamela Fishman (1983) women were active participants, usually followers rather than leaders, while the men acted as leaders or nonparticipants, but not as followers. Often women attempted to engage their male partners in a conversation but received only minimal response ("hmmm," "umm"). This resulted in female monologues punctuated by expectant but unfulfilled pauses. The women had to work harder to keep the conversation alive. Since one means of eliciting conversational participation is to ask questions, this tactic can result in the features observed by Lakoff: tag questions, and questions in place of statements (Fishman, 1980). As we noted before, these features can make the speaker look weak and unassertive.

The genderlect features described by Lakoff, Kramerae, West and Zimmerman, and Fishman all point to speech characterized as weak, tentative, hesitant, and trivial. For example, a tag question mitigates the assertive force of the statement it follows, apologies and self-deprecation lower the speaker's importance, and a participant's inability to control the topic of discourse relegates that participant to the role of perpetual follower and precludes the role of leader. In short, feminine genderlect is the speech of someone whose status is low.

We see, then, that what is actually being communicated by "genderlect" is not so much masculinity or femininity but relative amounts of status and power. Women who hold powerful or high status positions are not likely to use feminine genderlect in their professions. It is difficult to picture a female police officer saying, "Your driver's license expired last month, didn't it?" (with rising intonation) or the president of Smith College saying "We'll kind of have to strengthen our alumnae organizations across the country a little bit." Because women tend to hold lower status positions, they are more likely to use speech containing features of low powerlect, and these features of low powerlect have come to be identified as features of female genderlect.

The interaction of status and gender can be seen in nonverbal communication as well. Because of their smaller larynxes (and because of cultural influences: Mattingly, 1966; Sachs, Lieberman & Erickson, 1973), women have higher pitched voices. Higher pitched voices connote childhood rather than adulthood; and this connotation suggests lower status and power, for children are typically concerned with trivial matters, while adults are concerned with more serious matters; moreover, children are expected to defer to adults. Unsurprisingly, women who aspire to influential positions are often advised to cultivate lower pitched voices, voices that communicate authority. These women are also advised to speak louder, to project their voices. This contradicts the early socialization of many who were admonished as little girls to talk in a quiet, lady-like manner.

Because of their smaller physical size, women have smaller movements and take up less personal space. Albert Mehrabian (1981) postulated that implicit nonverbal communication conveys three fundamental messages: liking, interest, and status (or power). One of the external indicators of status is size. Bigger indicates more. A longer stride and larger gestures signify greater status. Needless to say, a larger person will naturally have a longer stride and larger gestures, even without socialization which reinforces and amplifies these differences. Women do, in fact exhibit a smaller stride and smaller gestures than men do, and socially prescribed feminine posture (crossed legs and hands in lap) promotes contraction rather than expansion of personal space (Bate, 1988; Eakins & Eakins, 1978; Henley, 1973/1974, 1977; Pearson, 1985, p. 252).

Mehrabian asserted that a second external indicator of status is relaxation. He noted that powerful animals such as bears and lions are able to relax much of the time, while less powerful animals like gazelles and rabbits must be alert much of the time. Mehrabian felt that the same is true of human beings. Higher status persons display more relaxed posture than do lower status persons, who display their attentiveness in posture and facial expression. Compared to the sitting, standing, and walking postures of men, women's postures are less relaxed, more attentive (Pearson, 1985, p. 252).

Attentiveness is communicated through eye contact and through smiling. Women give more eye contact and smile more than men do (Henley, 1973/1974; Muirhead & Goldman, 1979; Silveira, 1972; Thayer & Schiff, 1974). Eakins and Eakins postulated that people use eye contact (not mutual gazing) to get feedback on the appropriateness of their own behavior. The greater the eye contact, the more the person is seeking evidence of approval. Only a lower status person needs to be so concerned about approval. Eakins and Eakins have also noted that listeners are more likely to look at speakers than speakers look at listeners. Inasmuch as men seem to dominate mixed sex conversations, it is not surprising that women do more listening and therefore give more eye contact.

Women smile more than men do (Dierks-Stewart, 1979; Frances, 1979; Silveira, 1972). Not only does smiling indicate attentivenes, but Eakins and Eakins have suggested that smiling also indicates submission and approval seeking. Whether female smiling results from actual submissiveness and approval seeking or whether it is a socialized behavior, it conveys the message of lower status. Finally, Mehrabian noted that smiling is an indication of liking and interest. When a person's smiles are unreciprocated, when a person gives more attention than he/she receives, that person holds lower status.

This close relationship between gender and status has been investigated at length; the influence of a third factor, politeness, has not received as much attention (with the notable exception of Brown 1976, 1980, and Brown & Levinson 1978, 1980). But what is politeness? Brown and Levinson (1978) have decribed two fundamental politeness strategies: positive politeness strategies, which seek to affirm closeness and solidarity, and negative politeness strategies, which seek to show respect and to defer to the other's self-determination. Closely related to these strategies, and compatible with them, are Robin Lakoff's *Rules of Politeness*, later renamed *Rules of Rapport* (1973b, 1979):

1. Don't impose.
2. Give options.
3. Be friendly.

The first two (Don't impose, Give options) are negative politeness strategies, while the third (Be friendly) is a positive politeness strategy. If we were to interpret Lakoff's Rules of Politeness into specific behaviors, we would find several genderlect/powerlect features. We would find a set of instructions like this:

Don't Impose

   a) Be sure to soften your assertions with hedges, qualifiers, and tag questions; better yet, phrase your assertions as questions.

   b) Be sure to soften your requests by stating them as questions.

   c) Mitigate the full force of your opinions and feelings by expressing them with weak expletives and vague adjectives of approval or disapproval (preferably approval).

   d) Follow your partner's choice of topic of discourse; do not try to promote your own choice of topic (you may find that you will be ignored).

   e) Allow your partner ample time to talk, even if you must curtail the length of your own discourse; allow yourself to be interrupted, if need be.

f) Do not evoke strong feelings that could be unpleasant for your addressee; stick to trivial topics.

g) Keep your movements small and your posture constrained so that you will minimize your personal space and thereby grant more personal space to others.

h) Likewise, cultivate a quiet voice in order not to intrude upon the auditory space of others.

i) If you fail to observe any of the above suggestions, be sure to apologize and self-deprecate; better yet, apologize or self-deprecate from time to time, anyway (you might have unknowingly offended).

Give Options

a) Always state a request as a question; it gives your addressee more opportunity to decline.

b) Allow your addressee to control the topic of discourse so that he/she can choose what to talk about.

c) Allow yourself to be interrupted but do not interrupt your partner; this allows your partner to talk as much as he/she pleases.

Be Friendly

a) Be attentive in posture and in facial expression to show that you care about your addressee.

b) Give your addressee as much eye contact as you can; this shows your interest in your addressee and your desire to win his/her approval.

c) Most important, smile! There is no better way to indicate your liking for your partner.

If you have followed the above instructions, you have followed Lakoff's Rules of Politeness. You are a polite person.

These Rules of Politeness and their implementation are socially determined. It is not difficult to imagine the above instructions in a woman's magazine or in a how-to-be-popular book intended for women. It is more difficult to imagine these instructions appearing in a publication intended for a male audience.

The implementation of these rules is also culturally determined. Different cultures place varying degrees of emphasis upon each of these three rules. For example, in mainstream America, women are expected to follow Rule 1 (Don't impose) more closely than men are, hence the greater number of weak powerlect features in female genderlect. In upper- and middle-class England, however, both men and women are expected to avoid imposing. As a result, upper- and middle-class English men have features of weak powerlect in their speech, such as adjectives that mainstream Americans would consider feminine adjectives (Lakoff, 1973a, p. 53). Some Americans would consider these men to be overly polite and less masculine than American men. Of course, upper- and middle-class English men and women would consider these men to be polite and masculine.

Conversely, some cultures place less importance on Rule 1 than Americans do. Israeli men and women, for example, value friendliness and forthrightness and do not give as much attention to imposing or not imposing. The speech of these men and women contains direct assertions and requests without hedges and other mitigators. To mainstream Americans, Israeli men may seem forthright, sometimes impolite; to mainstream Americans, Israeli women may seem not only impolite, but also unfeminine. Of course, these women are neither impolite nor unfeminine to fellow Israelis (see Tamar Katriel's exploration of the "dugri" speech of native born Israelis, 1986).

In concluding our examination of gender, power, and politeness, we should consider the practical consequences of the interrelatedness of these three factors, specifically with regard to increasing the power of women -- not the power to dominate, but the power to achieve. This is the kind of power described by Bate (1988, pp. 39 and 40) and by Thorne, Kramerae, & Henley "power as energy, effective interaction, or empowerment" (1983, p. 19). This was the kind of power exercised by female students in a graduate seminar who empowered each other by using collaborative strategies; they did not divide a fixed commodity (power), but instead they created more.

Our specific concern is the interaction between people who are (or should be) equals. These interactions should be characterized by a reciprocated level of politeness. Thorne, Kramerae & Henley pointed out that polite, collaborative styles of communication are powerless only when they are not reciprocated (1983, pp. 18 and 19). It is in the interaction between equals that women can avoid overly polite, overly deferential forms of communication. This does not mean, however, that women should adopt a "masculine" style of communication; many women would be uncomfortable doing this and could be perceived negatively by others (Costrich, Feinstein & Kidder, 1975; Koester, 1982; Mills, 1985;

Scott, 1980; Wiley & Eskilson, 1982). We should avoid dichotomizing what is really a complex situation: One need not become superior in order to avoid being inferior, and one need not be impolite in order to avoid being powerless.

A person who understands the verbal and nonverbal features of genderlect/powerlect can communicate more flexibly and more effectively. For example, a woman who is being constantly interrupted by her addressee (who is interrupting not to affirm the woman's statements but to change the topic of discourse) need not become an interrupter, too. She can request that the interrupter stop interrupting or she can politely wait for the interrupter to finish, then ignore the attempted change of topic, and proceed with her ideas at the point of interruption, thereby maintaining her agenda of interests.

In short, by modifying her communicative behavior, a woman can influence the way others respond to her and she can begin to be the architect of her place in society.

NOTES

[1]Throughout this discussion of genderlect and powerlect, we should remember that we are not talking about dichotomous speech (masculine/feminine, weak/strong). Instead, we are talking about a continuum, along which a person's speech can be considered to be more or less stereotypically masculine or feminine, more less weak or strong.

REFERENCES

Adams, J. (1980). *Communication and gender stereotypes: An anthropological perspective.* Unpublished Ph.D. dissertation, University of California, Santa Cruz, CA.

Bailey, L.A., & Timm, L.A. (1976). More on women's -- and men's expletives. *Anthropological Linguistics, 18*, 438-49.

Bate, B. (1988). *Communication and the sexes.* New York: Harper & Row Publishers.

Brown, P. (1976). Women and politeness: A new perspective on language and society. *Reviews in Anthropology*, May/June, 240-49.

Brown, P. (1980). How and why women are more polite: Some evidence from a Mayan community. In S. McConnell-Ginet, R. Borker, & N. Furman (Eds.), *Women and language in literature and society* (pp. 111-36). New York: Praeger.

Brown, P., & Levinson, S. (1978). Universals in language usage: Politeness phenomena. In E. Goody (Ed.), *Questions and politeness: Strategies in social interaction* (pp. 56-289). Cambridge: Cambridge University Press.

Brown, P., & Levinson, S. (1980). Social structure, groups, and interaction. In K.R. Scherer and H. Giles (Eds.), *Social markers in speech* (pp. 291-341). Cambridge: Cambridge University Press.

Costrich, N., Feinstein, J., & Kidder, L. (1975). When stereotypes hurt: Three studies of penalties for sex-role reversals. *Journal of Experimental Social Psychology, 11*, 520-30.

Crosby, F., & Nyquist, L. (1977). The female register: An empirical study of Lakoff's hypotheses. *Language in Society, 6*, 313-22.

Dierks-Stewart, K. (1979). Sex differences in nonverbal communication: An alternative perspective. In C.K. Berryman & V.K. Eman (Eds.), *Communication, language, and sex: Proceedings of the first conference* (pp. 112-21). Rowley, MA: Newbury House Publishers.

Dubois, B.L., & Crouch, T. (1975). The question of tag questions in women's speech: They don't really use more of them, do they? *Language in society, 4*, 289-94.

Eakins, B., & Eakins, R. (1978). *Sex differences in human nonverbal communication.* New York: Houghton-Mifflin Company.

Fishman, P. (1980). Conversational insecurity. In H. Giles, W.P. Robinson, & P.M. Smith (Eds.), *Language: Social psychological perspectives* (pp. 127-32). New York: Pergamon Press.

Fishman, P. (1983). Interaction: The work women do. In B. Thorne, C. Kramarae, & N. Henley (Eds.), *Language, gender and society* (pp. 89-101). Rowley, MA: Newbury House Publishers.

Frances, S.J. (1979). Sex differences in nonverbal behavior. *Sex Roles, 5*, 519-535.

Hartman, M. (1976). A descriptive study of men and women born in Maine around 1900 as it reflects the Lakoff hypotheses in language and woman's place. In B.L. Dubois & I. Crouch (Eds.), *The sociology of the languages of American women* (pp. 81-90). San Antonio: Trinity University.

Hartman, M. (1978). Sex roles and language. Paper presented to the 9th World Congress of Sociology, Uppsala, Sweden.

Henley, N. (1973/1974). Power, sex and nonverbal communication. *Berkely Review of Sociology, 18*, 1-26. Also in B. Thorne and N. Henley (Eds.), *Language and sex: Difference and dominance* (pp. 185-203). Rowley, MA: Newbury House Publishers.

Henley, N. (1977). *Body politics: Power, sex and nonverbal communication.* Englewood Cliffs, NJ: Prentice-Hall.

Katriel, T. (1986). *Talking straight: "Dugri" speech in Israeli Sabra culture.* New York: Cambridge University Press.

Koester, J. (1982). The Machiavellian princess: Rhetorical dramas for women managers. *Communication Quarterly, 30*(3), 165-72.

Kramarae, C. (1974). Women's speech: Separate but equal? *Quarterly Journal of Speech, 60*, 14-24.

Kramarae, C. (1981). *Women and men speaking: Frameworks for Analysis.* Rowley, MA: Newbury House Publishers.

Kuykendall, E. (1980). Breaking the double binds. *Language and Style,* 81-93.

Lakoff, R. (1973). *The logic of politeness, or minding your P's and Q's.* Papers from the Ninth Regional Meeting of the Chicago Linguistic Society, University of Chicago.

Lakoff, R. (1973a). Language and women's places. *Language in Society, 2,* 45-80.

Lakoff, R. (1979). Stylistic strategies within a grammar of style. In J. Orasanu, M. Slater, & L.L. Adler (Eds.), *Language sex, and gender* (pp. 53-78). New York: Annals of the New York Academy of Sciences.

Mattingly, I. (1966). Speaker variation and vocal-tract size. Paper given at Acoustical Society of America.

Mehrabian, A. (1981). *Silent messages: Implicit communication of emotions and attitudes* (2nd ed.). Belmont, CA: Wadsworth Press.

Metts, S., & Bryan, G. (1984). Politeness: A conversational indicator of sex roles. Presented at Central States Association Convention, Chicago.

Muirhead, R.D., & Goldman, M. (1979). Mutual eye contact as affected by seating position, sex, and age. *The Journal of Social Psychology, 109,* 201-206.

O'Barr, W. (1982). Speech styles in the courtroom. Chapter 5 of *Linguistic evidence: Language, power, and strategy in the courtroom.* New York: Academic Press.

Pearson, J. (1985). *Gender and communication.* Dubuque, IA: Wm. C. Brown.

Sachs, J., Lieberman, P., & Erickson, D. (1973). Anatomical and cultural determinanats of male and female speech. In R. Shuy and R. Fasold (Eds.), *Language attitudes: Current trends and prospects* (pp. 74-84). Washington, DC: Georgetown University Press.

Scott, K.P. (1980). Perceptions of communication competence: What's good for the goose is not good for the gander. *Women's Studies International Quarterly, 3,* 199-208.

Silveira, J. (1972). *Thoughts on politics of touch* (Volume 1). Eugene, OR: Women's Press.

Spender, D. (1980). *Man made language.* London: Routledge & Kegan Paul.

Thayer, S., & Schiff, W. (1974). Observer judgement and social interaction: Eye contact and relationship inferences. *Journal of Personality and Social Exchange, 30,* 110-114.

Thorne, B., Kramarae, C., & Henley, N. (1983). *Language, gender, and society.* Rowley, MA: Newbury House Publishers.

Valian, V. (1977). Linguistics and feminism. In M. Vetterling-Braggin, F.A. Elliston, and J. English (Eds.), *Feminism and philosophy* (pp. 154-66). Totowa, NJ: Littlefield, Adams.

West, C. (1979). Against our will: Male interruptions of females in cross-sex conversation. In J. Orasanu, M. Slater, & J. Adler (Eds.), *Language, sex, and gender* (pp. 81-100). New York: Annals of the New York Academy of Sciences.

West, C., & Zimmerman, D. (1983). Small insults: A study of interruptions in cross-sex conversations between unacquainted persons. In B. Thorne, C. Kramarae & N. Henley (Eds.), *Language, gender, and society* (pp. 103-17). Rowley, MA: Newbury House Publishers.

Wiley, M.G., & Eskilson, A. (1982). Coping in the corporation: Sex role constrains. *Journal of Applied Social Psychology, 12*(1), 1-11.

Zimmerman, D., & West, C. (1975). Sex roles, interruptions, and silences in conversation. In B. Thorne & N. Henley (Eds.), *Language and sex: Difference and dominance*. Rowley, MA: Newbury House Publishers.

SYNOPSIS . . . . .

Nancy Hoar's exploration of the mutual effects of gender, power, and politeness upon communication is continued in Frances Sayer's examination of the relationships between power and biological sex, sex role, and conversational competence. Sayers notes the confusion and contradiction found in previous studies that examined these relationships, and has attempted to untangle this confusion.

Sayers has chosen an approach which combines self-evaluation on the Bem Sex-Role Inventory and on Cegala's Interaction Involvement Scale with video-taped conversations of male-female pairs of strangers. What is most notable about this study is not the disambiguation that Sayers was seeking (and did not find), but her analysis of the mixed outcome of her correlations. First, she points out that it is not so much the number of interruptions or overlaps in a conversation that should concern us, but the reason for these interruptions and overlaps. Sayers points out that some interruptions and overlaps are confirming responses rather than attempts to commandeer the conversation. This should not surprise us, we have probably noticed and given such responses in the everyday conversations we participate in; but many of us have not incorporated this observation into our systematic investigations of communication.

Sayers also notes that questions need not be attention-getters or conversation facilitators, but they can also be a means of controlling a conversation. So, while it may be a person whose conversation is laced with questions could be doing what Fishman (1978) calls the "shitwork" of interaction, it may just as well be that this person is dominating the conversation. We will not know if we only count the number of questions in a conversation. Look too at the content and purpose of the questions.

Finally, Sayers shows us the need for exploring what the observed conversational behaviors actually mean to the participants. It is risky practice, indeed, for the investigator to infer what a speaker actually intended, without consulting the speaker. Included in this exploration of speaker intent should also be an assessment of the speaker's knowledge of communication stereotypes and strategies. Sayers acknowledges the problems which inevitably emerge when we study the communication of people who themselves are students of communication (most often the readily available undergraduates in our own classes).

In short, Sayers has demonstrated that detached observation alone is not enough. An investigator must take into account the content and context of the communication, as well as the participant's knowledge and intent. Sayers maintains that we should broaden our methodology; for example, we should be ready to use interpretation and introspection. We should be more creative in our investigative techniques.

Fran Sayers

SEX, SEX-ROLE AND CONVERSATION

REVIEW OF THE LITERATURE AND RATIONALE

Recently, researchers, educators, management trainers and newswriters have focused on sex differences in communication behaviors and how they influence interaction. A number of forces in our society have made the need to understand similarities and differences in both the ways women and men view their world and in specific everyday behaviors. The women's movement, issues of equal opportunity, the entrance of more women into the workplace, and our greater representation at higher levels of business and professional endeavor have made understanding between friends, lovers and colleagues of different sex a necessity.

A considerable volume of recent research on how females and males communicate appears to stem, at least in part, from frequently cited hypotheses set forth by Lakoff (1975) which propose that men and women use different language patterns and that the language conventions serve to maintain a "woman's place. " Also during the mid-197Os, research reports and summaries cataloged behaviors which show men dominating conversations by controlling the opportunity to speak and women providing support for this pattern of interaction (see, for example, Eakins & Eakins, 1978; Henley, 1977; Zimmerman & West, 1975). Whether men dominate and women defer is a continuing debate. Two sets of characteristics, one more concerned with relationships and aesthetic values and the other task-oriented, apparently exist in communication behavior, in fact, in any successful, satisfying human activity. Whether the communication behaviors discussed by the writers above can be categorized either by the dominance/deference or the relationship/task paradigm and whether the same behaviors are used more frequently by one sex than the other remains unclear. Furthermore,researchers are beginning to give attention to whether the meaning intended and perceived attached to such conversation management behaviors as interruptions and listener responses varies according to situation,sex or other factors.

At least three bodies of research confirm that in our society two sets of characteristics and functions are used and considered ideal. Further, these sets of traits can be sorted into masculine and feminine quite consistently when rating speech samples or describing an ideal person. First, Bakan's (1966) theoretical development of the idea of agent and communion, Parsons and Bales'

Fran Sayers is a Consultant and Trainer with Resources Unlimited, P.O. Box 6638, Portland, Maine 04101.

(1955) concern with instrumentality and expressiveness, and Bales' (1950) emphasis on the need for task groups to include people playing two different sets of roles all tap into the same two categories. Similar sets of descriptor terms appear in analyses of gender-blind ratings of speech transcripts and in empirical test development discussed below.

Second, Martin and Craig (1983) reviewed three studies in which subjects evaluated written transcripts of female and male speakers with all gender cues removed. In each case the females received higher ratings on aesthetic quality, and the males on such characteristics as dynamism, aggression and confidence.

Third, the developers of tests of masculinity and femininity (Bem, 1974; Berzins et al., 1978; Heilbrun, 1976; Spence et al., 1975) derived their test items by empirical sorting procedures to determine the characteristics associated with the ideal male and female. Items for masculinity scales (MS) and femininity scales (FS) derived by this method parallel the two sets of qualities assigned to females and males in sex-blind studies and in the test-development studies. That is, the ratings of males, whether actual or ideal, contain characteristics which fit Bakan's idea of "agency" and Parson and Bales' idea of "instrumentality" (e.g., dynamic, assertive, aggressive, acts like a leader). Likewise, the female qualities (e.g., affectionate, sensitive to the needs of others, aesthetic, etc.) fit the theoretical constructions "communion"and "expressiveness." Ickes points out (1981) that the convergence of similar sets of traits is strong evidence of the validity of both the theoretical and the data-based conclusions. Therefore, we see that the traits assigned to speakers of unknown sex, the traits assigned to the "ideal"male and female in empirical test item development and the theoretical propositions concerning the important traits for the functioning of human beings individually and in groups consistently fall into two categories labeled masculine and feminine. Closely related to these three groups of research findings are assertions that certain linguistic and paralinguistic behaviors are used more frequently by one sex and, further, that these behaviors maintain the status and power structure of this society.

Much of the literature **can** be interpreted to support the idea that males use various speaking and listening behaviors to control conversation and that females are especially supportive and deferent in cross-sex interaction (LaFrance & Mayo, 1979). This interpretation appears to fit the pattern of masculine characteristics being more instrumental and female characteristics more expressive. On the other hand, a number of researchers have more recently reported results which do not show a difference in the behaviors interpreted to indicate dominance by males and deference by females. Reviews have appeared in the literature periodically(see, for example, LaFrance & Mayo, 1979; Martin & Craig, 1983). We have chosen here to outline the literature in Table 1.

Newcombe & Arnkoff 's (1979) study analyzed ratings of male and female "powerful" and "powerless" speech. The study (which included courtroom, business and social settings) showed the use of qualifiers elicited higher ratings on

TABLE 1

DO SUPPORT SEX-LINKED DEFERENCE/DOMINANCE PATTERN

Speaker Behaviors
Amount of Speech. Males speak more (Strodtbeck, 1951; Strodtbeck, et al, 1957; Hilpert, et al, 1957; Argyle et al., 1968; Duncan & Fiske, 17, 1977) and use more filled pauses while speaking (Duncan & Fiske, 1977).

Interruptions. Males interrupt more (Zimmerman & West, 1975; West & Zimmerman, 1977; Eakins & Eakins, 1978; West, 1979; McMillan, et al, 1977).

Qualified Language or Feminine Register (Crosby & Nyquist, 1977). Females use more tag questions, hedges and qualifying words, intensifiers, overly polite forms, more questioning intonation, more compound requests (Lakoff, 1973; Smeltzer & Watson, 1986).

Statements, Questions and Topic Control. Males make more declarative statements, challenge partner's statements and generally control topic. Females ask more questions (Fishman, 1978) and make more supportive statements (Bohn & Stutman, 1983).

Vocabulary Use. Females use greater variety of descriptor terms (Lakoff, 1973), talk more about people and use many self- and partner-referent pronouns (Gleser et al., 1959; Hirschman, 1974).

Eye Behavior. Females look at their partner more (Duncan & Fiske, 1977).

Listener Behaviors
Audible Response to Speaker. Females use more "supportive back-channels." Males are more likely to use "delayed minimal response" (Zimmerman & West, 1975) and show lack of enthusiasm (Fishman, 1978).

Inaudible Response to Speaker. Females look at partner and smile more (Duncan & Fiske, 1977).

DO NOT SUPPORT SEX-LINKED DEFERENCE/DOMINANCE PATTERN

Speaker Behaviors
Amount of Speech. No sex difference was found in amount of speech (Hirschman, 1973; Markel et al., 1976; McMillan et al. , Martin & Craig, 1983; Kennedy & Camden, 1983; Fitzpatrick & Dindia, 1986).

Interruptions. No sex difference was found in interruptions (Martin & Craig, 1983 Kennedy & Camden, 1983; Dindia, 1987).

Qualified Speech or Feminine Ratio Behaviors. No sex difference was found in intonation patterns (Edelsky, 1979), tag questions (Dubois & Crouch, 1975) or qualifiers (Martin & Craig, 1983).

Statements. Females offer more nonsupporting statements (appears similar to challenge of partner's statement) (Bohn & Stutman, 1983).

warmth and compound requests received higher ratings on warmth and politeness than simple requests. Bradley's (1981) study showed women losing in the ratings on dynamism, knowledge and intelligence more than their male counterparts when they used qualified language. Studies designed to estimate the influence of speech style in the courtroom (Bradac et al. , 1981; Lind & O'Barr, 1979; Warfel, 1984; Wright & Hosman, 1983) produced mixed results. In general, the more powerful speaker was considered more dynamic, competent, trustworthy, attractive, credible and convincing. However, exceptions to this pattern included women in Wright & Hosman' s study whose high frequency of intensifiers elicited high ratings on attractiveness. Taken together, these studies show that linguistic patterns do influence person perception but not in a linear relationship with evaluation variables.

Given then, that reactions to different speech styles vary, neither powerful nor powerless speech is effective in every situation. Thus, a need for flexibility in speech behavior provides further support for the theoretical propositions of Bakan (1966) and Parsons and Bales (1955) that both aspects of human nature and behavior are crucially important. Bem (1974) and others (Berzins et al., 1978; Heilbrun, 1976; Spence et al., 1975) saw this state of having both types of characteristics, agency and communion, task-orientation and relationship-orientation,integrated in the same person as desirable and labeled the concept androgyny. They developed tests consisting of masculine and feminine subscales to measure the constructs feminine and masculine sex-typed and androgyny. We will limit our discussion to the Bem Sex-Role Inventory (BSRI).

Bem based her test and concept development on the idea that each person has some qualities stereotypically associated with their own sex and the opposite sex. Further, individuals have these characteristics to various degrees and some people of both sexes possess a sufficient degree of masculine and feminine traits to be called androgynous. Bem reasoned that an androgynous person would be more adaptive and effective in interaction than sex-typed persons. Other researchers have attempted to validate her theoretical proposition.

Wheeless and Duran (1982) concluded from comparisons of self-report tests that their androgynous subjects were more adaptive and more competent in conversation. Attempts to relate subjects' behavior in conversation to their BSRI scores and their adaptability have produced mixed results. Researchers have compared at least two groups of behaviors to sex-role: a group of behaviors which serve to reinforce the partner and regulate the speaking turn (Dittman, 1972; Knapp, 1978) and a group of paralinguistic and linguistic behaviors showing uncertainty, including tag questions, statements ending in a rising inflection, hedges and empty adjectives. These behaviors were grouped together and labeled Feminine Register by Crosby & Nyquist (1977). Studies comparing sex-role (BSRI) to selected reinforcing/regulating behaviors (e.g., smiling, gazing, interruptions and pausing behavior in conversation) suggest androgyny and, in some cases, femininity (LaFrance & Carmen, 1981) is associated with adaptability and competence in conversation (Ickes, 1981; LaFrance, 1981). In a comparison between Feminine Register behaviors and sex-role, Crosby et al. (1981), the feminine females showed greater adaptability. Although the use of different behavioral variables and apparently somewhat different meanings for "adaptability"render the research results difficult to interpret, androgyny and femininity appear to have complex links with the ability to play the role of conversational partner in a variety of situations. This ability to be interdependent with a variety of specific others in verbal and nonverbal interaction is the focus of a recent effort to develop a test of competence in conversation.

Cegala and his colleagues developed and validated a self-report test, "Interaction Involvement Scale" (IIS) (Cegala, 1980; Cegala et al. , 1982) with a theoretical basis in Goffman's ideas of "line" and "face."Goffman (1967) stressed the need to maintain a "line" which is a pattern of verbal and nonverbal behavior used to express one's view of the situation and evaluation of the interactants. The maintenance of a "line" makes it possible to establish "face" which is the social value or territory which a person stakes out for him/herself by the line others perceive he or she takes. The interactive nature of conversation or the interdependence of people to "make it happen" is the focus of interest here. The IIS taps into dimensions of responsiveness, perceptiveness, and attentiveness. Responsiveness is defined as the overt behaviors of delivering appropriate lines in conversation. Perceptiveness is a measure of covert behavior or the individual's view of self and interactive partner in the milieu created by the interaction. Attentiveness items measure one's alertness to conversational cues especially those of the interactional partner. The total test is probably a self-assessment of competence in conversation.

How does this relate to sex-role stereotyping? The subjects in the Cegala et al. (1982) study who were classified as androgynous on the BSRI showed high scores on the Perceptiveness items of the IIS. Why the androgynous subjects did not show high scores on the entire IIS is not clear. Another confusing point is that feminine sex-typed subjects did not show high scores on attentiveness. Inasmuch as feminine items on BSRI include such characteristics as "sympathetic" and "sensitive to the needs of others," a connection between FS and IIS scores seems a reasonable expectation. The ability to be a partner to "making it happen" in conversation appears equivalent to adaptability in specific interactions and closely related to attentiveness and "sensitivity to the needs of others."

In an investigation of nonverbal behaviors associated with the IIS, Cegala et al. (1982) paired subjects of the same sex with one partner high on IIS and the other low. They found that males with high IIS scores showed more eye gaze and females more partner-focused gesturing. These various results were obtained by different research designs and comparison is confusing. However, taken together they do seem to suggest possible connections among scores on the BSRI, the IIS and conversational behavior. Whether measurement of sex-role or conversational competence will be refined to be more accurate predictors of behavior than biological sex is still an open question.

PURPOSE OF THE STUDY

This analysis is an effort to explore relationships among the MS and FS respectively of the BSRI, sex, the IIS and the Speaker Behaviors which appear in Table 1. The primary interest was to discover whether these behaviors often associated with dominance and power can be predicted more accurately by biological sex, sex-role as measured by BSRI, or by a measure of conversational competence, the IIS. Due to the conflicting results of earlier research, no predictions were made concerning the behaviors of interest.

METHOD

Sample
The subjects were volunteers from first year and sophomore-level communication classes at a small New England university. They formed 18 previously unacquainted cross-sex dyads. Their mean age was 21.4 years, and 27 of the 36 subjects were sophomores and freshmen.

Procedures
A research assistant met the volunteers in a classroom and asked them to complete the IIS and the BSRI and then escorted them to a studio for taping. The studio was set up with chairs and a table with coffee and doughnuts. The researcher greeted them and asked them to talk and get acquainted and invited them to help themselves to the refreshments. The researcher had informed them when they volunteered that their conversation would be audio- and videotaped. Taping was done through a one-way mirror. This analysis is based on the first ten minutes of the audiotapes.

Data Analysis
The IIS was scored to produce one score by reversing poles on the items which showed a negative loading on the factor analysis in the validation studies (Cegala et al. 1982) and computing the average. Scoring the IIS as three scores (attentiveness, responsiveness, and perceptiveness) has considerable theoretical advantage in a larger sample, but in a sample this size the need to improve subject to variable ratio took precedence. For the same reason, sample size, statistical analysis would not be meaningful if the sample were divided into four groups by their scores on the BSRI. Following Crosby et al. (1981), separate scores were used in this analysis: a masculinity (MS) and a femininity (FS) scale.

Trained assistants timed the amount of speech (VS) using electronic stopwatches for one subject at a time. All subjects' speech was timed by two assistants. A comparison of their work showed differences did not exceed two seconds in any case.

A preliminary inspection of the tapes showed that subjects did not use polite forms, compound requests, specialized descriptors, and challenges of partner's statement. Three coders counted interruptions (INT), questions (Q), tag questions (TQ), statements ending with a rising inflection (SRI), qualifiers and hedges (H), intensifiers or empty adjectives (IEA), and the ungrammatical use of "so" (SO) (using so as an intensifier to other descriptors). When counts were discrepant, two coders listened to the tapes again together, reviewed the definitions of variables and made a judgment on the count.

Following a pattern begun by Crosby and Nyquist (1977) and most recently used by Crosby et al. (1981), a score was computed which collapsed several behaviors hypothesized by Lakoff to be typical of women's speech into a Feminine Register (FR). In this study FR includes TQ, SRI, H, IEA, and SO.

Ratios per ten minutes were computed for variables obtained by frequency count to adjust for different total speaking times and to obtain a higher level of data. FR and Q were converted to a ratio of subject's own amount of speech (FRR and RQ, respectively). Interruptions were converted to a ratio (RINT) of interruptions to the partner's amount of speech. The following formula was used for conversion:

Ratio = Frequency of behavior/(Amount of speech x 10)

Separate Pearson Product Moment Correlations tables were generated for females and males to compare IIS, MS, FS, amount of speech (VS), RINT, RQ and FRR. Oneway Analyses of Variance were used to test whether females and males differed in RINT, RQ, and FRR. The behavioral variables were compared to the self-report tests by Pearson Product Moment Correlation. Tables were generated for the variables IIS, MS, FS, VS, RINT, RQ and FRR.

RESULTS

The Analyses of Variance showed that there was a statistically significant difference between the sexes on amount of speech and questions but not on interruptions or FRR. The comparisons of amount of speech showed a consistent tendency for the males to speak more ($F = 73.5$, $p = .001$, $R = 68$). The mean amount of speech in minutes was: females, 3.60, $SD = .652$; and males, 5.27, $SD = .505$.

Ratios of interruptions to the partner's amount of speech did not differ significantly for males and females ($F = .05$, $p = .82$, $R = .002$). The means were: females, .078, $SD = .053$ and for males, .74. The frequency count of interruptions showed males with slightly higher count, 5.27, and females with 4.11. The higher ratio for females is a function of the male partner's greater amount of speech.

Females asked significantly more questions than males ($F = 12.7$, $p = 001$, $R = .27$). The mean ratio of questions to amount of speech was: females, .280, $SD = .135$ and for males, .145, $SD = .086$.

The females showed more FR behaviors and a slightly higher FRR. The mean ratios for females were .443, $SD = .214$, and for males, .335, $SD = .147$. However, the difference was not significant ($F = 3.1$, $p = .09$, $R = .09$).

The females' IIS scores correlated with their MS ($r = 5216$, $p = .013$) but not FS scores ($r = .0906$, $p = .360$). The males showed strong positive correlations between IIS and MS ($r = .6298$, $p = .002$) and between IIS and FS ($r = .3984$, $p = .050$).

Correlations among the self-report tests and the observed behaviors were not statistically significant. For the females the IIS and MS showed a trend toward inverse correlation with RINT ($r = .3526$, $p = .075$ and $r = -.3462$, $p = .079$). For the males, a trend was found toward positive correlation between RQ and MS ($r = .3321$, $p = .089$) and a negative trend between RQ and FS ($r = -.3195$, $p = .098$).

The males' behaviors did not show meaningful intercorrelations. For the females, RQ was negatively correlated ($r = .4157$, $p = .043$) with RINT and showed a positive trend toward positive correlation with FRR ($r = .3322$, $p = .089$).

DISCUSSION

The results of this study lend very limited support to the position that men are dominant and women deferent in conversation in that men spoke and interrupted more and women asked more questions. The relationships among the IIS, MS, and FS and the conversational behaviors studied suggest some trends for further investigation.

The consistent pattern of more speech by males in the conversations analyzed here adds to the confused state of research results on this issue. Other studies which show men using more of the speaking time in conversation were published between 1950 and 1977. Studies showing females and males sharing the speaking time were published from 1973 to 1986 (see Table 1). The use of speaking time by the students in this study was similar to the subjects in the earlier group. (This study is based on data collected in 1983.)

Researchers have focused considerable attention on interruptions. The earlier literature created an impression that males in general habitually interrupt females in conversation and, further, that this behavior is an indication of dominance. This study does not support that position. The frequency counts of interruptions by females were higher than for males; the males spoke more. Thus, it seems that the males had less opportunity and the females more opportunity to break into the partner's conversation.

Kennedy and Camden (1983) provide a fresh way to look at interruptions. They categorized interruptions in small task-oriented groups and found that over half of the interruption behavior served to confirm the previous speaker. Their study of the interruptions and the pre- interruption speeches in no way supported the idea that interruptions are behaviors which show dominance. Their work should serve to direct study of interruptions as an integral part of interactions which have multiple functions. Their subjects were graduate students; we could speculate that graduate students are probably different in their approach to a group task from undergraduates and the general public. Whether that is the case or not, the approach has merit. Future study should focus both on what variables surround the interruption behavior and on how interruptions may be used and reacted to constructively.

At least two explanations for the lack of a significant difference in submissive or nonassertive conversational behaviors (FRR) between females and males seem plausible. First, these behaviors may simply not be the habit of females in general; or the behaviors of the FR may occur less often when college students engage in cross-sex conversation. Sex did not prove to be a reliable predictor of FR in the Crosby et al. (1983) and the Martin and Craig (1983) studies which used college students as subjects. Crosby and Nyquist (1977) found that a difference in FR was accounted for by role (public or police officer) rather than by sex. Further clouding the issue is Martin and Craig's finding that male subjects used fewer qualifying words in social conversations when speaking to females than to males. Clearly, the use of such nonassertive behaviors as qualified speech is not solely the domain of females.

The women in this study asked more questions than the men. As might be expected in get-acquainted conversations, virtually all questions by both sexes were requests for information about the partner. Questions can be used to control a conversation (Folger & Sillars, 1980) or to draw the other person out (Soskin & John, 1963). In these conversations, questioning was used primarily but not exclusively for the latter purpose. Women simply used this method for encouraging the partner to talk more often than the men did. Fishman (1978) asserts that women do the "shitwork of conversation." Women and men in this study shared the work of keeping the conversation going. If frequency of questions which encourage the partner to talk is an index, women took on more of this work.

The correlations among the self-report scales may be a function of the subjects' perception of what is acceptable or "good." The women in the study who rated themselves highly in conversational competence (IIS) also ascribed traditional male characteristics to themselves (MS). Given the frequent discussion of differing characteristics and behaviors of the sexes in the media and in the university where these data were collected, such a result is not surprising. A number of female students have expressed dismay to this researcher upon hearing the tape of discussion in which they participated and realizing that they use the FR behaviors. They may have a similarly negative connotation for some of the characteristics included in the feminine scale of BSRI. Take for example, "yielding"and "flatterable." Although they may be sufficiently yielding to enjoy an easygoing conversation, they may not be willing to think of themselves as yielding or flatterable.

The desire to appear acceptable or attain an ideal may also explain the high correlation between the three tests for males. Visual inspection of data indicate these three scores correlate positively because they are all high. Interaction with male students and recent media reports substantiate our belief that male students generally wish to have the qualities included in the MS and FS scales (for example, see the report in USA Today, November 5, 1984, based on a poll of their readers conducted by Gordon S. Black Corporation).

The self-report tests, IIS, MS and FS do not relate strongly to the conversational behaviors of interest. The females' negative correlation trend between IIS and MS and RINT may be related to confidence in their ability to handle the conversation smoothly. That is, if they saw themselves as high on the characteristics related to task-orientation and on the conversation management behaviors tested in the IIS, they may not have found it necessary to interrupt their partner to get their ideas across. Further study of interruptions in these data and in other samples may shed light on this connection. The relationships among the males' questioning behavior and the MS and FS will require a different approach. Question like interruptions apparently serve a variety of functions in conversation. Counts and ratios of questions are inadequate for understanding. Research conducted in a variety of circumstances and contexts will be necessary to sort out the variables which reliably predict these paralinguistic behaviors.

Sex of the speaker (Wright & Hosman, 1983) and the context of the interaction(Warfel, 1984) have been shown to influence the raters' perceptions of qualified language. Experience confirms that tag questions can give a variety of impressions. Consider these examples: One spouse says to the other, "We'll have dinner at six, right?" or the boss says to the employee the day before a holiday, "You will come in tomorrow,won't you?" Thus, while we might reasonably infer a pattern of dominance/submission in both conversations sampled, the person using the tag question would be labeled submissive in the first case and dominant in the second.

At least two major challenges to researchers remain in gender-related behavior: first, to continue the effort to unearth reliable predictors of conversational behavior, and second, to investigate how effective different conversational behaviors are in goal accomplishment. We should keep in mind that the goals of participants may include many facets of relationship maintenance and task accomplishment. One aspect of goal accomplishment is awareness of the possibility of incongruency in the perception of meanings; i.e., conversational partners may assign different meanings to specific behaviors. For example, evidence suggests that supportive back channels may be interpreted differently by females and males (see Crosby et al., 1983).

A number of scholars have made appeals for pursuing gender-related research from a variety of viewpoints and using a wide spectrum of research methods (see, for example, Goodall, 1984; Ickes, 1981; Jackson, 1984; Pearce & Freeman, 1984). Goodall proposed that analysis of personal experience related to gender issues has been neglected. He suggests that we who do research should delve into our own experiences and apply theoretical knowledge to this data which we understand better than that which we collect from others. Johnson (1984) delved into her own experience in professional contexts to analyze a few examples of descriptive language used by males and to comment on how analysis of personal experiences is one valid way of knowing. An analysis of how the results of this study compare to the personal experiences of the author in cross-sex interactions in academic and other settings is underway.

In summary, as we use a variety of research methods to broaden our base for information-gathering,we should also study the possible interaction effects of other factors with gender. The coming years should produce some interesting and useful insights both in cataloging conversational behavior and in discovering ways to aid those who wish to make their communications more effective in accomplishing their purpose.

NOTES

[1]Powerful speech in these studies employs straightforward, unqualified statements. Powerless speech is qualified speech which includes tag questions, hedges or qualifiers and, in some cases, intensifiers.

[2]Ickes refers to adapatability to the conversation partner's sex-role; the other three studies apply adaptability to the difference in instrumental and expressive conditions.

[3]BSRI scores were not reported for this study. Subjects were selected from the original study in which subjects classified as androgynous by the BSRI had higher scores on the perceptiveness factor of the IIS.

REFERENCES

Argyle, M., Lalljee, M., & Cook, M. (1968). The effects of visibility on interaction in a dyad. *Human Relations, 21,* 3-17.

Bakan, D. (1966). The duality of human existence. Boston: Beacon. Bales, R. (1950). *Interaction process analysis: A method for the study of small groups.* Cambridge, MA: Addison-Wesley.

Bate, B. (1984). Submerged concepts in gender communication research. *Women's Studies in Communication*, *7*, 101-104.

Bem, S. (1974). The measurement of psychological androgyny. *Journal of Consulting and Clinical Psychology*, *42*, 155-162.

Bem, S. (1977). On the utility of alternative procedures for assessing psychological androgyny. *Journal of Consulting and Clinical Psychology*, *45*, 196-205.

Berzins, J.I., Welling, M.A., & Wetter, R.E. (1978). A new measure of psychological androgyny based on the personality research form. *Journal of Consulting and Clinical Psychology*, *46*, 126-138.

Bohn, E. , & Stutman, R. (1983). Sex-role differences in the relational control dimension of dyadic interaction. *Women's Studies in Communication*, *6*, 96-104.

Bradac, J. , Hemphill, M. , & Tardy, C. (1981). Language style on trial: Effects of "powerful" and "powerless" speech upon judgments of victims and villains. *The Western Journal of Speech Communication*, *45*, 327-341.

Bradley, P. (1981). The folk-linguistics of women's speech: An empirical examination. *Communication Monographs*, *48*, 73-90.

Cegala, D. (1981). Interaction involvement: A cognitive dimension of communicative competence. *Communication Education*, *30*, 109-121.

Cegala, D. , Savage, G. , Brunner, C. , & Conrad, A. (1982). An elaboration of the meaning of interaction involvement : Toward development of a theoretical concept. *Communication Monographs*, *42*, 229-294.

Crosby, F. , Jose, P. , & Wong-McCarthy, W. (1981). Gender, androgyny, and conversational assertiveness. In C. Mayo & N. Henley (Eds.), *Gender and nonverbal behavior* (pp. 151-170). NY: Springer-Verlag.

Crosby F., & Nyquist, L. (1977). The female register: An empirical study of Lakoff's hypothesis. *Language in Society*, *6*, 313-322.

Dindia, K. (1987). The effects of sex of subject and sex of partner on interruptions. *Human Communication Research*, *13*, 345-371.

Dittmann, A. (1972). Developmental factors in conversational behavior. *The Journal of Communication*, *22*, 404-423.

Dubois, B. , & Crouch, I. (1975). The question of tag questions in women's speech: They don't really use more of them, do they? *Language in Society*, *4*, 289-294.

Duran, R., & Wheeless, V. (1980). Social management: Toward a theory based operationalization of communication competence. Paper presented to the Speech Communication Association convention.

Eakins, B. , & Eakins, G. (1976). Verbal turn-talking and exchanges in faculty dialogue. In B.L. Dubois & I. Crouch (Eds.), *The sociology of the languages of American women* (pp. 53-62). San Antonio, TX: Trinity University.

Eakins, B. , & Eakins, G. (1978). *Sex differences in human communication.* Boston: Houghton Mifflin.

Fishman, P.M. (1978). Interaction: The work women do. *Social Problems, 25,* 397-406.

Fitzpatrick, M., & Dindia, K. (1987). Couples and other strangers: Talk time in spouse-stronger interaction. *Communication Research, 13,* 625-652.

Folger, J. , & Sillars, A. (1980). Relational coding and perceptions of dominance. In B. Moore & L. Phelps (Eds.), *Interpersonal communication: A relational perspective.* Minneapolis: Burgess.

Goffman, E. (1967). *Interaction ritual: Essays in face-to-face behavior.* Chicago: Aldine Publishing Co.

Goodall, H., Jr. (1984). Research priorities for investigations of gender and communication: Rediscovering the human experience of sexuality and talk. *Women's Studies in Communication, 7,* 91-97.

Gumperz, J.J. (1977). Sociocultural knowledge in conversational inference. In M. Saville-Troike (Ed.), *Linguistics and anthropology.* Washington, DC: Georgetown University Press.

Haas, A. (1979). Male & female spoken language differences: Stereotypes & evidence. *Psychological Bulletin, 86,* 616-626.

Heilbrun, A.B. (1976). Measurement of masculine and feminine sex role identities as independent dimensions. *Journal of Consulting and Clinical Psychology, 44,* 183-190.

Henley, N. (1977). Body politics: Power, sex and nonverbal communication. Englewood Cliffs, NJ: Prentice-Hall.

Hilpert, F. , Kramer, C. , & Clark, C. (1975). Participants' perceptions of self and partner in mixed-sex dyads. *Central States Speech Journal, 26,* 52-56.

Hirschman, L. (1973). Female-male differences in conversational interaction. Paper presented to the Linguistic Society of America convention, San Diego, CA.

Ickes, W. (1981). Sex-role influences in dyadic interaction: A theoretical model. In C. Mayo & N. Henley (Eds.), *Gender and nonverbal behavior* (pp. 95-128). NY: Springer-Verlag.

Kennedy, C,, & Camden, C. (1983). A new look at interruptions. *Western Journal of Speech Communication, 47,* 45-58.

Knapp, M. (1978). *Nonverbal communication in human interaction* (2nd ed.) (pp. 353-354). NY: Holt, Rinehart, & Winston.

Kramer, C. (1975). Women's speech: Separate but unequal? In B. Thorne & N. Henley (Eds.), *Language and sex: Difference and dominance* (pp. 41-56). Rowley, MA: Newbury House Publishers.

Jackson, L. (1984). Available research methods to study gender role in communication. *Women 's Studies in Communication, 7,* 86-90.

Johnson, F. (1984). Positions for knowing about gender differences in social relationships. *Women's Studies in Communication, 7,* 77-82.

LaFrance, M. (1981). Gender gestures: Sex, sex-role and nonverbal communication. In C. Mayo & N. Henley (Eds.), *Gender and nonverbal behavior* (pp. 129-150). NY: Springer-Verlag.

LaFrance, M. , & Carmen, B. (1980). The nonverbal display of psychological androgyny. *Journal of Personality and Social Psychology, 38,* 36-49.

LaFrance, M. , & Mayo, C. (1979). A review of nonverbal behaviors of women and men. *The Western Journal of Speech Communication, 43,* 96-107.

Lakoff, R. (1975). *Language and woman's place.* NY: Harper Colophon Books.

Lind, E. , & O'Barr, W. (1979). The social significance of speech in the courtroom. In H. Giles & R. St. Clair (Eds.), *Language and social psychology (pp. 66-87). Baltimore: University Park Press.*

Markel, N., Long, J., & Saine, T. (1976). Sex effects in conversational interaction: Another look at male dominance. *Human Communication Research, 2,* 356-364.

Martin, J. , & Craig, D. (1983). Selected linguistic sex differences during initial social interactions of same-sex and mixed-sex student dyads. *Western Journal of Speech Communication, 47,* 16-28.

Newcombe, N. , & Arnkoff, D. (1979). Effects of speech style and sex of speaker on person perception. *Journal of Personality and Social Psychology, 37,* 1293-1303.

Parsons, T., & Bales, R. (1955). Family, socialization, and interaction processes. NY: Free Press of Glencoe.

Pearce, W.B., & Freeman, S. (1984). On being sufficiently radical in gender research: Some lessons from critical theory, Kang, Milan, and MacIntyre. *Women's Studies in Communication, 7,* 65-68.

Smeltzer, L., & Watons, K. (1986). Gender differences in verbal communication during negotiations. *Communication Research Reports, 3,* 74-79.

Soskin, W., & John, V. (1963). The study of spontaneous talk. In R. Barker (Ed.), *The stream of behavior.* NY: Appleton-Century-Croft.

Spence, J.T., & Helmreich, R.L. (1975). Masculinity and femininity. Austin: University of Texas Press.

Spence, J.T., Helmreich, R. , & Stapp, J. (1975). Ratings of self and peers on sex role attributes and their relation to self-esteem and conceptions of masculinity and femininity. *Journal of Personality and Social Psychology, 32,* 29-39.

Strodtbeck, F. (1951). Husband-wife interaction over revealed differences. *American Sociological Review, 16,* 468-473.

Strodtbeck, F., & Mann, R. (1956). Sex role differentiation in jury deliberations. *Sociometry, 19,* 3-11.

Warfel, K. (1984). Gender schemas and perceptions of speech style. *Communication Monographs, 51,* 253-267.

Wheeless, V. , & Duran, R. (1982). Gender orientation as a correlate of communicative competence. *The Southern Speech Conmunication Journal, 43,* 51-64.

Wright, J., & Hosman, L. (1983). Language style and sex bias in the courtroom: The effects of male and female use of hedges and intensifiers on impression formation. *The Southern Speech Communication Journal, 48*, 137-152.

Zimmerman, D., & West, C. (1975). Sex roles, interruptions and silences in conversation. In B. Thorne & N. Henley (Eds.), *Language and sex: Difference and dominance* (pp. 105-129). Rowley, MA: Newbury House Publishers.

SYNOPSIS.....

Constance Staley, like Frances Sayers, advocates an expanded frame of reference for studying communication. Staley is concerned with the application of communication strategies in business and management and has examined the literature of managerial communication to find the efficacy of communication strategies characterized by varying degrees of power, strategies characterized as feminine or as masculine. Her ultimate concern is the specification of effective managerial training programs.

The expanded frame of reference advocated by Staley requires that we consider how others evaluate a communicative style, not just how they perceive it. Many of the studies examined by Staley show that women managers are faced with a "double bind," that is, they can use a communicative style that is perceived as powerful and effective per se, but which is evaluated as less acceptable and therefore less effective when used by women. Or, these women can use what is perceived to be a more feminine style, which is evaluated as more socially appropriate, but less effective in a managerial setting. Staley acknowledges that stereotypes are strong influencers of both perception and evaluation.

In dealing with the perceptual and evaluative factors that put women managers in this double bind, Staley offers a very practical, common sense approach: don't focus on styles, focus on results. Simply because respondents in a study of managerial communication evaluate a particular style as ineffective or unacceptable, we should not assume that the user of this style is an ineffective manager. The real question is: Does the person get results? If yes, then the manager is effective, and style is of secondary concern.

Constance Courtney Staley

The Communicative Power of Women Managers: Doubts, Dilemmas, and Management Development Programs

Although the rate at which women have moved into prestigious careers has been slower than predicted in the early years of the women's movement, there is evidence to suggest that such a transition is taking place. Between 1970 and 1978, for example, the rate at which women moved into managerial-administrative positions increased 16 times more rapidly than during the previous 20 years (White, DeSanctis, & Crino, 1981, p. 549). This change indicates a general drive toward equal participation by males and females at top levels of management; however, researchers, trainers, and a watchful public share a concern for women's satisfaction and their effectiveness in these positions (Staley, 1984, p. 317).

To that end, the last ten years have been characterized by prolific advice to the woman manager--advice which, in short, suggests that the way to succeed in male-dominated corporations is to **speak up** (Kintzing, 1979; Korda, 1977; Stone & Bachner, 1977; West, 1982). Similarly, she has been advised to "play the game" (Harragan, 1977), to "dress for success" (Harragan, 1977; Korda, 1977; Molloy, 1977), and to "seize power and wield clout" (Kennedy, 1980).

Recently, however, this single-minded voice of many management "trainers" has come under close scrutiny. Koester (1982), for example, identified a prominent theme emerging from many popular self-help books--the Machiavellian princess. The woman manager must, first and foremost, overcome her biggest handicap--"the woman herself" (Lynch, quoted in Koester, 1982, p. 166). Furthermore, the entire burden of negativism or discrimination must be shouldered by the female professional:

> If she is unable to change their (others') assessment of women in general and herself in particular, she is responsible. The obvious difficulty in changing attitudes and behaviors of other people means that the woman accepting the tenet that she is in control of her own fate will repeatedly come face-to-face with failure. (Koester, 1982, p. 169)

Beyond such self-help advice, the last fifteen years have also been characterized by in-house and off-site management development training programs for women. Many programs have been sex-segregated in order to allow women an

Constance Staley is an Associate Professor at the University of Colorado, Colorado Springs, Colorado.

opportunity to speak freely, without feeling defensive or intimidated in the presence of men, and to compare experiences with their female colleagues (Carter, 1980). As one expert puts it, "Business schools and executive-development programs are male designed, male oriented and male taught. . . . however, management methods that work well for men in a male environment cannot be adopted wholesale by women because **women managers get a different response from co-workers**" (Harragan, 1984, p. 38). According to this view, women's management challenges are specific to women, and training programs should address this fact of life.

On the other hand, many experts are sharply critical of management training programs designed exclusively for women, resenting their remedial and patronizing bias and their potential to perpetuate myths about women managers (e.g., Berryman-Fink & Fink, 1985; White, 1981; Wood & Conrad, 1983). Curricula of such programs often emphasize "woman-related problems in business, with only an 'overview' of management principles being discussed" (Carter, 1980, p. 22). Furthermore, some experts note, despite their underlying philosophy, many programs for women counterproductively promote imitation of male behaviors. Recent research verifies the belief that women may be perceived negatively when they behave according to traditionally masculine styles (Haccoun, Sallay, & Haccoun, 1978; Wiley & Eskilson, 1982). Some program administrators note that sex-segregated programs are dying out while others still report strong enrollments (Spruell, 1985, p. 33).

Regardless, according to some, the future calls for a new style of management, one characterized by a blending of male (task-oriented) and female (people-oriented) styles (e.g., Berryman-Fink & Fink, 1985; Sargent, 1983). Less optimistic experts agree in theory with androgynous management as an ideal. Practically speaking, however, they see such changes as slow in coming--if at all-since organizations generally opt for efficiency and, often, the status quo (Spruell, 1985, p. 33; Yarbrough, 1984a). One prominent female professional, Katherine Graham, simply cautions women to be patient:

> Career-minded women haven't been in the work force long enough yet to have gained the experience for top management. "When they reach their 40s and 50s, they will have earned the right to do the truly creative work, make the big decisions and have the most impact--in other words, exercise power." (Spruell, 1985, p. 31)

The purpose of this review is to examine current representative literature in order to elucidate remaining doubts about the communicative power the woman manager can wield, to underscore dilemmas of power and influence she faces yet, and to comment on how management development programs for the next decade should respond.

The Communicative Power of Women

Although Jesperson first characterized the speech of women as weak, dull, and empty in 1922, it was feminist linguists of the 1960s and 1970s who first expressed concern over the communicative power of women. Lakoff (1973) and Key (1975) were among the first to assert that women use language which trivializes content, disguises assertions, and projects--and perpetuates--a subordinate position in society. As Wiley and Eskilson (1985) summarize, "Many of the dimensions on which male and female speech are believed to differ reflect the power of the speaker" (p. 994).

Furthermore, early research indicated that not only might a woman communicate hesitantly through such linguistic forms as word choice, intonation, and syntax, but her communicative power was often eroded by her conversational partner, particularly if that partner was male (e.g., Eakins & Eakins, 1978; Fishman, 1978; Zimmerman & West, 1975).

Early folk-linguists, as they have been named (Bradley, 1981; Kramer, 1974a), such as Key (1975) and Lakoff (1973), prompted researchers to attempt verification of their assertions. Few resulting studies document the actual existence of "women's language" (e.g., Crosby & Nyquist, 1977; McMillan, Clifton, McGrath, & Gale, 1977; Mulac, Lundell, & Bradac, 1986), while other studies report findings of no differences (Crawford & Chaffin, 1987; Rubin & Nelson, 1983; Smeltzer, & Werbel, 1986). Although later renamed "powerless language" since both females and males can communicate a lack of involvement and power (O'Barr & Atkins, 1980), such linguistic forms appear to generate a stronger negative response when used by female speakers. In a study by Bradley (1981), for example, women in mixed-sex groups who advanced their arguments with disclaimers and tag questions exerted little influence and were seen as having little knowledge and intelligence. Males, however, who used these linguistic forms were not devalued by other group members.

On the other hand, a larger body of research supports the existence of a **perceived** "women's language" (see, for example, the works of Berryman-Fink & Wilcox, 1983; Edelsky, 1976; Kramer, 1974a, 1974b, 1977, 1978; Liska, Mechling & Stathas, 1981; Quina, Wingard, & Bates, 1987; Siegler & Siegler, 1973). Kramer (1977, p. 159) found that female speech, in contrast to the speech of males, is perceived as "kind, correct--but unimportant" and ineffective. More recently, Quina, Wingard, and Bates (1987) reported that the stereotypical female speech style--language which includes hedging, incomplete sentences, indirect statements, a lack of expletives, expressiveness, use of tag questions, full description (vs. brevity), indirect requests, illogical connectors, indecisiveness, undifferentiated adjectives, and overgeneralization--is perceived as more socially warm, but less competent. They summarized: "A polite, warm linguistic style is not consistent with the popular image of American corporate success or achievement" (p. 118).

In other words, while research demonstrates that women's speech is stereotypically preferred as more **interpersonally** competent communication (e.g., Kramer, 1977; Scott, 1980), it is also perceived as less **professionally** competent communication. Krasner, Snodgrass and Rosenthal (1984) found that males were rated as significantly more professionally competent than females by their tone of voice alone. In a more recent study, Steckler and Rosenthal (1985) found that females' voices were rated as sounding more verbally and nonverbally competent when speaking with their bosses, while males' voices were rated as more competent when talking to their peers. The authors speculate that either consciously or unconsciously, a woman may attempt to sound more "competent" when communicating to those most likely to doubt her competence: "She may make a special effort to compensate to impress upon her boss that she is businesslike and competent, contrary to established stereotypes of women" (p. 162).

Findings such as these uncover a potential dilemma for women:

> Women find themselves in a double bind in which if they exhibit the language behavior rated more effective than that used by men, they may still be viewed as less effective because females are perceived as having less power and influence. If they convey a style linked with male stereotypic characteristics, they may be viewed as unfeminine and also unable to be effective in communication. (Scott, 1980, p. 207)

The Communicative Power of Women Managers

While much research focuses on the communicative power of women in general, few studies characterize the communicative potential of female professionals. A number of studies would lead us to believe that males and females perform similarly in organizations, particularly, in such substantive areas as leadership behavior (Bartol, 1977; Day & Stogdill, 1972; Osborn & Vicars, 1976), potential management capability (Bass, Krusell, & Alexander, 1971), and preferred conflict style (Shockley, 1981; Shockley-Zalabak & Morley, 1984). In fact, in a large-scale, multifaceted study of nearly 2000 male and female managers' managerial philosophy, motivation to work, participative practices, interpersonal competence, and management style, Donnell and Hall (1980) found only two overall differences. They reported that female managers' work motivation profiles were more achieving and, directly relating to communication, females were less open and candid with their colleagues (p. 8). Subordinates of female managers also reported that they solicited less feedback from their superiors than did subordinates of male managers (p. 7).

Along these lines, Birdsall (1980) found that male and female managers communicated similarly during staff meetings, in terms of providing rules information, fact information, value information, control, support, play, and authority reference. As Miner (1973) summarized, "Women appear to manage well for essentially the same reasons men do--that is, existing criteria for excellence are equally appropriate for both" (p. 148). Current literature indicates that many such criteria are based in communication competence (e.g., Beam, 1981; DiSalvo, 1980; DiSalvo, Larson, & Seiler, 1976; Goldhaber, 1983; Naisbitt, 1982; Phillips, 1982).

In this vein, recent research indicates that a female professional's self and supervisor assessments of communication proficiency are critically important to organizational advancement. In their recent work, Shockley-Zalabak, Staley, and Morley (1988) found that supervisor evaluation of seven communication competencies accounted for 55% of the variance in promotions for female professionals. Interestingly, however, a female professional and her supervisor may not agree on the woman's level of proficiency in such communication areas as interviewing, giving oral presentations, using communications technology, group decision-making, handling interpersonal relationships, motivating people, delegating authority, business writing, diagnosing organizational problems, listening, negotiating, handling grievances, demonstrating leadership/management techniques, managing conflict, and giving directions. Although previous research has demonstrated that the perceptions of subordinates and superiors can differ (e.g., Baird, 1977; Henemann, 1974; Thornton, 1968), in a recent study of female professionals specifically, Staley and Shockley-Zalabak (1986) found that females and their supervisors agreed in only three of the fifteen competency areas above, and that females as a group rated themselves as more competent than supervisors as a group rated their female subordinates in twelve of fifteen communication competency areas. Similarly, in assessing training needs for female professionals in each of the fifteen areas, agreement between females and their supervisors was found in only four areas.

Therefore, beyond the question of the actual extent or quality of the female professional's communication assets lies the critical question of how those assets are evaluated. Hollander and Julian (1979) point out that the most important factor in determining the selection of potential managers and leaders may not be actual or even perceived behavior, but rather, how behavior is evaluated. Although the literature includes a myriad of results, research on sex effects in evaluation indicates that the level of performance involved is one of three primary factors underlying sex bias in evaluation (Nieva & Gutek, 1980). In their extensive review, for example, Nieva and Gutek report the work of Haefner (1977) who surveyed employers and found that while they made little distinction in selecting between a barely competent employee of either sex, they clearly preferred to hire highly competent males over highly competent females. Likewise, Rosen and Jerdee (1974) found a strong pro-male bias in demanding jobs requiring decisive action and aggressive interpersonal behavior. Highly competent females, according to Nieva and Gutek's review of existing literature, are more likely than males to experience discriminatory bias in evaluation and are less likely than males to be rewarded for their successes. Furthermore, because of sex-role stereotyping, a woman's successful performance is often attributed to effort, task ease, or luck, rather than ability (Deaux, 1976; Deaux & Emswiller, 1974; Feldman-Summers & Kiesler, 1974).

Along these lines, Bradley (1980) found that task competent women who argued for deviate positions in mixed-sex groups were influential, but they were not viewed as positively as their male counterparts. Regardless, she attributed their ability to influence successfully to a "surprise factor": men are expected to display competence, but a competent female, on the other hand, must be "extraordinary" and therefore may be dealt with as "something other than a female" (p. 110). Other researchers label this positive response to competent females the "talking platypus phenomenon" (Abramson, Goldberg, Greenberg, & Abramson, 1977) or explain similar findings analagously by referring to Samuel Johnson's famous remark of the eighteenth-century: "Sir, a woman preaching is like a dog's walking on his hind legs. It is not done well; but you are very surprised to find it done at all" (Jacobson & Effertz, 1974, p. 393). In other words, while research indicates that highly competent females, as opposed to highly competent males, may be discriminated against in performance evaluations, other studies note that extra-competent females are sometimes labeled remarkable and therefore successfully skirt (no pun intended) traditional biases.

Doubts and Dilemmas Facing Women Managers

Current representative literature reveals not only reservations about the communicative power a woman manager can wield, but research also underscores several potential dilemmas of power and influence she may face (Staley, 1986).

According to research, for example:

1. If women speak as research indicates they are **perceived** to speak, their speech may be seen as ideal, yet ineffective (Kramer, 1977, 1978; Scott, 1980). Standing alone, this body of research suggests that speaking like a woman may represent a debilitating handicap, particularly in organizational contexts.

2. If women, in particular, speak "women's language," negative sanctions follow (Bradley, 1981), yet if women are trained to use "power language," negative assessments may also result. According to Wiley and Eskilson's 1982 study, "attempts to reduce bias by training women to employ a masculine interaction style will not reduce unequal evaluations" (p. 8). In their research published in 1985, they report that "acting as men act (or talking as men do), while it may lead to imputations of success and power, will apparently result in negative evaluations. . ." (p. 1005). Furthermore, they note that females, as opposed to males, are much more sensitive to variations in verbal style. Since males still occupy most positions of

control in organizations, evaluations of individuals may not be affected by their choice of speech. They suggest:

> Unless women are represented in the upper echelons of corporations or men in such positions are sensitized to vari- ations in verbal style, training women to use powerful styles of speech in order to achieve success in management may be an empty gesture. (p. 1004)

3. More generally, if women imitate masculine styles, they may not be seen as effective (Haccoun et al., 1978). According to Wiley and Eskilson (1982), **reward** power is seen as an effective style for women to employ, as compared to **expert** power which is more appropriate for men. Reward power, however, is less desirable since it requires surveillance for compli- ance and is therefore unreliable (French and Raven, qtd. in Wiley and Eskilson, 1982). Results such as these are even more ironic when viewed alongside accumulating evidence which notes few substantive differences between male and female managers in many areas of performance. Re- gardless of the number of actual differences that exist, perceived differ- ences and stereotyped expectations may still override the evidence.

4. Even if women work to improve their communication competence through training, they may find that their superiors disagree with their assessments of their own proficiency (Staley & Shockley-Zalabak, 1986). Furthermore, by increasing overall competency, the question remains: Do women also run the risk of increasing the possibility of discriminatory evaluation? (Nieva and Gutek, 1980)

In short, the weight of evidence suggests that women managers face doubts about their communicative power--some self-imposed perhaps, and some the result of cultural attitudes which lag behind current realities. More importantly, beyond such doubts lie dilemmas elucidated in representative research, dilem- mas concerning communicative power and managerial training for the female professional.

Management Development Programs for the 1990S

The research discussed above generates numerous questions for women managers and for management trainers. **Can** professional women communicate powerfully, or are they doomed to the dilemmas elucidated through research? How **should** women managers communicate in order to experience satisfaction and success? What types of training curricula would best serve the needs of the woman manager of the nineties?

In the last twenty years, we have witnessed increasing numbers of women entering the work force and larger proportions of women achieving managerial positions. As Spruell (1985) reports, however, "not all women are pleased with how high they have climbed, and not all of them blame themselves" (p. 33). In a 1985 *Harvard Business Review* survey of business executives, the majority of male respondents and three-quarters of female respondents reported that a woman must still be exceptional to succeed in the business world (Sutton & Moore, 1985); consequently "many women who have managerial potential but do not strike others as being exceptional may never be given the opportunity they deserve to demonstrate their capabilities" (p. 50). Similarly, one *HBR* respondent out of three expressed a belief that women will never be completely accepted in the world of business.

We find ourselves in times of transition, and while the trend may be away from women-only training programs, many of the challenges facing women managers remain. Obviously, all working women do not develop professionally at equivalent rates, nor do they start from the same place; therefore, some women may still need women-only training programs in order to "catch up." Moreover, limited political awareness among women in organizations--probably best remedied in women-only training groups--remains a significant stumbling block (Yarbrough, 1984b).

Regardless, the trainer of the present and of the future, must remain focused on an operational definition of communicative power for woman managers. **Powerful** communication is not simply a stylistic variant of **powerless** communication. Powerful communication is communication that **works**, communication that brings action, influence, results. Perhaps more is done to ensure communicative power when women in management development programs are provided with substance to communicate powerfully **about**--first, when the focus is on management skills such as oral and written communication, leadership, decision making ability, organization and planning; and second, when the cultivation of task competence, whatever that may be for individual women, is emphasized. In other words, as women reach "maturity" in the work force, communicative power may evolve over time as a natural by product of task competence and well developed managerial skills. Regardless of whether training opportunities are segregated or integrated, it is these abilities, in the superlative, which may overcome doubts and dilemmas by triggering Bradley's "surprise factor." Conversely, superficial strategies such as teaching assertive or powerful communication first, and even foremost, and skills and competence second--as many programs have emphasized in the past--may represent a "backwards" orientation.

Perhaps managers of the 1990s will be androgynous. Perhaps she or he-- they--will be better prepared to meet **all** the requirements of effective management. Perhaps management trainers can guide women and men toward this ideal. Between now and then, perhaps the woman manager will begin to realize that while the full burden of responsibility for the attitudes and behaviors of others is **not** solely her responsibility, she must continue to develop substantive bases for her communicative power.

Likewise, trainers must rely on research in order to recognize far-reaching problems and to create farsighted programs. The gap between theory and practice may be narrowed through a solid grounding in a broad base of current literature. By the same token, having this knowledge at one's disposal aids in developing program content which is at the center of contemporary analysis.

BIBLIOGRAPHY

Abramson, P. R., Goldberg, P. A., Greenberg, J. H., & Abramson, L. M. (1977). The talking platypus phenomenon: Competency ratings as a function of sex and professional status. *Psychology of Women Quarterly, 2,* 114-124.

Baird, L. S. (1977). Self and superior ratings of performance: As related to self-esteem and satisfaction with supervision. *Academy of Management Journal, 20*(2), 291-300.

Bartol, K. M. (1977). *Male versus female leaders: A review of comparative literature.* Syracuse, NY: School of Management.

Bass, B. M., Krusell, J., & Alexander, R. A. (1971). Male managers' attitudes toward working women. *American Behavioral Scientist, 15,* 221-236.

Beam, H. H. (1981). Good writing: An underrated executive skill. *Human Resource Management, 20,* 2-7.

Berryman-Fink, C., & Fink, C. B. (1985). Optimal training for opposite sex managers. *Training and Development Journal, 39*(2), 26-29.

Berryman-Fink, C., & Wilcox, J. R. (1983). A multivariate investigation of perceptual attributions concerning gender appropriateness in language. *Sex Roles, 9*(6), 663-681.

Birdsall, P. (1980). A comparative analysis of male and female managerial communication style in two organizations. *Journal of Vocational Behavior, 16,* 183-196.

Bradley, P. H. (1980). Sex, competence and opinion deviation: An expectation states approach. Communication Monographs, 47(2), 101-110.

Bradley, P. H. (1981). The folk-linguistics of women's speech: An empirical examination. *Communication Monographs, 48*(4), 73-90.

Carter, J. (1980). New directions needed in management training programs for women. *Texas Business Executive, 6*(1), 22-24, 27.

Crawford, M., & Chaffin, R. (1987). Effects of gender and topic on speech style. *Journal of Psycholinguistic Research, 16*(1), 83-89.

Crosby, F., & Nyquist, L. (1977). The female register: An empirical study of Lakoff's hypotheses. *Language in Society, 6,* 313-322.

Day, D. R., & Stogdill, R. M. (1972). Leader behavior of male and female supervisors: A comparative study. *Personnel Psychology, 25,* 353-360.

Deaux, K. (1976). Sex: A perspective on the attribution process. In J. H. Harvey, W. J. Ickes, & R. F. Kidd (Eds.), *New directions in attribution research.* Hillsdale, NJ: Erlbaum.

Deaux, K., & Emswiller, T. (1974). Explanations of successful performance on sex-linked tasks: What is skill for the male is luck for the female. *Journal of Personality and Social Psychology, 29,* 80-85.

DiSalvo, V. (1980). A summary of current research: Identifying communication skills in various organizational contexts. *Communication Education, 29,* 283-290.

DiSalvo, V., Larson, D. C., & Seiler, W. J. (1976). Communication skills needed by persons in business organizations. *Communication Education, 25,* 269-275.

Donnell, S.M., & Hall, J. (1980). *Men and women as managers: A significant case of no significant differences.* The Woodlands, TX: Telemetrics International.

Eakins, B. W., & Eakins, G. (1978). *Sex differences in human communication.* Boston, MA: Houghton-Mifflin.

Edelsky, C. (1976). The acquisition of communicative competence: Recognition of linguistic correlates of sex roles. *Merrill-Palmer Quarterly, 22* (1), 47-59.

Feldman-Summers, S., & Kiesler, S. B. (1974). Those who are number two try harder: The effect of sex on social attrbiutions of causality. *Journal of Personality and Psychology, 30* (6), 846-855.

Fishman, P. M. (1978) Interaction: The work women do. *Social Problems, 25* (4), 397-406.

Goldhaber, G. M. (1983). *Organizational communication.* Dubuque, IA: Wm. C. Brown.

Haccoun, D. M., Sallay, G., & Haccoun, R. R. (1978). Sex differences in .the appropriateness of supervisory styles: A nonmanagement view. *Journal of Applied Psychology, 63,* 124-127.

Haefner, J. E. (1977). Sources of discrimination among employees: A survey investigation. *Journal of Applied Psychology, 62* (3), 265-270.

Harragan, B. L. (1977). *Games mother never taught you: Corporate gamesmanship for women.* New York: Rawson Associates.

Harragan, B. L. (1984). Management training for women. *Working Woman, 9*(2), 38.

Henemann, H. G. (1974). Comparison of self and superior ratings of managerial performance. *Journal of Applied Psychology, 59,* 638-642.

Hollander, E. P., & Julian, J. W. (1979). Contemporary trends in the analysis of the leadership process. *Psychological Bulletin, 71* (5), 387-397.

Jacobson, M. B., & Effertz, J. (1974). Sex roles and leadership: Perceptions of the leaders and the led. *Organizational Behavoir and Human Performance, 12,* 383-396.

Jesperson, O. (1922). *Language: Its nature, development, and origin.* London: Allen & Unwin.

Kennedy, M. M. (1980). *Office politics: Seizing power and wielding clout.* Chicago: Warner Books.

Key, M. R. (1975). *Male/female language.* Metuchen, NJ: Scarecrow.

Kintzing, J. (1979, March). Psyching up for speaking up. *Mademoiselle,* p. 15.

Koester, J. (1982). The Machiavellian princess: Rhetorical dramas for women managers. *Communication Quarterly, 30*, 165-172.

Korda, M. (1977). *Success: How every man and woman can achieve it.* New York: Random House.

Kramer, C. (1974a, June). Folklinguistics. *Psychology Today*, pp. 82-85.

Kramer, C. (1974b). Women's speech: Separate but unequal? *Quarterly Journal of Speech, 60*, 14-24.

Kramer, C. (1977). Perceptions of female and male speech. *Language in Speech, 20*, 151-161.

Kramer, C. (1978). Women's and men's ratings of their own and ideal speech. *Communication Quarterly, 26*, 2-11.

Krasner, S. Q., Snodgrass, S. E., & Rosenthal, R. (1984, May). *Is the executive woman an oxymoron? Tone of voice and the evaluation of executive competence.* Paper presented at the meeting of the International Communication Association, San Francisco, CA.

Lakoff, R. (1973). Language and woman's place. *Language in Society, 2* (1), 45-80.

Liska, J., Mechling, E. W., & Stathas, S. (1981). Differences in subjects' perceptions of gender and believability between users of deferential and nondeferential language. *Communication Quarterly, 29*, 40-48.

McMillan, J. R., Clifton, A. K., McGrath, D., & Gale, W. S. (1977). Women's language: Uncertainty or interpersonal sensitivity and emotionality? *Sex Roles, 3* (6), 545-559.

Miner, J. B. (1973). The real crunch in managerial manpower. *Harvard Business Review, 51* (6), 146-158.

Molloy, J. T. (1977). *The women's dress for success book.* New York: Warner Books, Inc.

Mulac, A., Lundell, T. L., & Bradac, J. J. (1986). Male/female language differences and attributional consequences in a public speaking situation: Toward an explanation of the gender-linked language effect. *Communication Monographs, 53* (2), 115-129.

Naisbitt, J. (1982). *Megatrends: Ten new directions transforming our lives.* New York: Warner Books.

Nieva, V. F., & Gutek, B. A. (1980). Sex effects on evaluation. *Academy of Management Review, 5* (2), 267-276.

O'Barr, W. M., & Atkins, B. K. (1980). "Women's language" or "powerless language"? In R. Borker, N. Furman, and S. McConnell-Ginet (Eds.), *Women and language in literature and society* (pp. 93-110). New York: Praeger.

Osborn, R. N., & Vicars, W. M. (1976). Sex stereotypes: An artifact in leader behavior and subordinate satisfaction analysis? *Academy of Management Journal, 19*, 439-449.

Phillips, G. (1982). *Communicating in organizations.* New York: Macmillan Pulbishing Company.

Quina, K., Wingard, J. A., & Bates, H. G. (1987). Language style and gender stereotypes in person perception. *Psychology of Women Quarterly, 11*, 111-122.

Rosen, B., & Jerdee, T. H. (1974). Effects of Applicant's sex and difficulty of job on evaluations of candidates for managerial positions. *Journal of Applied Psychology, 59* (4), 511-512.

Rubin, D. L., & Nelson, M. W. (1983). Multiple determinants of a stigmatized speech style: Women's language, powerless language, or everyone's language? *Language and Speech, 26* (3), 273-290.

Sargent, A. G. (1983). *The androgynous manager.* New York: AMACOM.

Scott, K. P. (1980). Perceptions of communication competence: What's good for the goose is not good for the gander. *Women's Studies International Quarterly, 3,* 199-208.

Shockley, P. S. (1981). The effects of sex differences on the preference for utilization of conflict styles of managers in a work setting: An exploratory study. *Public Personnel Management, 10*(3), 289-295.

Shockley-Zalabak, P. S., & Morley, D. M. (1984). Sex differences in conflict styles preferences. *Communication Research Reports, 1*(1), 28-32.

Shockley-Zalabak, P., Staley, C. C., & Morley, D. D. (1988). The female professional: Communication proficiencies as predictors of organizational advancement. *Human Relations, 41*(7), 553-567.

Siegler, D. S., & Siegler, R. (1973). *Stereotypes in male and female speech.* (ERIC Document Reproduction Service No. ED 120 657)

Smeltzer, L. R., & Werbel, J. D. (1986). Gender differences in managerial communication: Fact or folk-linguistics? *Journal of Business Communication, 23*(2), 41-50.

Spruell, G. (1985). Making it, big time--is it really tougher for women? *Training and Development Journal, 39*(8), 30-33.

Staley, C. (1984). Managerial women in mixed groups: Implications of recent research. *Group & Organization Studies, 9* (3), 316-332.

Staley, C. (1986). Gender and communication research: deliberations, dilemmas and directions. *The Pennsylvania Speech Communication Annual, 17,* 29-35.

Staley, C., & Shockley-Zalabak, P. (1986). Communication proficiency and future training needs of the female professional: Self-assessment versus supervisors' evaluations. *Human Relations, 39* (10), 891-902.

Stekler, N. A., & Rosenthal, R. (1985). Sex differences in nonverbal and verbal communication with bosses, peers, and subordinates. *Journal of Applied Psychology, 70*(1), 157-163.

Stone, J., & Bachner, J. (1977). *Speaking up: A book for every woman who wants to speak effectively.* New York: McGraw-Hill.

Sutton, C. D., & Moore, K. K. (1985, September-October). Executive women--20 years later. *Harvard Business Review,* pp. 42-44, 48, 50, 52, 56, 58, 60, 62, 66.

Thornton, G. C. (1968). The relationship between supervisory and self-appraisals of executive performance. *Personnel Psychology, 21* (4), 441-455.

West, C. (1982). Why can't a woman be more like a man? *Work and Occupations, 9*(1). 5-29.

White, M. C., DeSanctis, G., & Crino, M. D. (1981). Achievement, self-confidence, personality traits, and leadership ability: A review of literature on sex differences. *Psychological Reports, 48*(2), 547-569.

White, P. (1981). Do women managers still need special training? *Training, 18*(9), 102-110, 115.

Wiley, M. G.. & Eskilson, A. (1982). Coping in the corporation: Sex role constraints. *Journal of Applied Social Psychology, 12*(1), 1-11.

Wiley, M. G., & Eskilson, A. (1985). Speech style, gender stereotypes, and corporate success: What if women talk more like men? *Sex Roles, 12*(9-10), 993-1007.

Wood, J. T., & Conrad, C. (1983). Paradox in the experiences of professional women. *Western Journal of Speech Communication, 47*(4), 305-322.

Yarbrough, E. (1984a, February). *Men and women working together: A critique.* Paper presented at the meeting of the Western Speech Communication Association, Seattle, WA.

Yarbrough, E. (1984b, February). *Political awareness for women in organizations.* Paper presented at the meeting of the Western Speech Communication Association, Seattle, WA.

Zimmerman, D.H., & West, C. (1975). Sex roles, interruptions and silences in conversation. In B. Thorne & N. Henley (Eds.), *Language and sex: Difference and dominance* (pp. 105-129). Rowley, MA: Newbury House.

SYNOPSIS . . . . .

Carol Ann Valentine and Banisa Saint Damian seem to pursue a somewhat alternate direction by looking at the perceptions of the voice and how the gender of the speaker and the speaker's culture affect perceptions of communicative power. One result is a clarity that the "ideal voice" is not a woman's voice.

Within cultures, in Mexico, the ideal male voice and female voices corresponded closely on dimensions of pitch, volume, rate and diction. In the United States, though neither the male nor the female voice conformed completely to the ideal, the ideal male conformed more closely to the cultural ideal.

The ideal speaker's voice in Mexico and the United States shows the qualities of clear enunciation and cheerfulness, while being well-modulated and free of regional accent. The ideal male voice in both cultures was expected to be somewhat low in pitch and somewhat slow. However, the ideal Mexican male was expected to use greater volume and take more care with diction than the United States' male.

The ideal female voice types in Mexico and the United States were similarly described as soft in volume, medium to somewhat slow in rate of delivery, and careful in enunciation. However, the ideal Mexican female voice was additionally expected to be delicate and sensual.

Upon closer inspection, we see that the Valentine and Saint Damian study actually does not pursue an alternative direction. They, too, are talking about Staley's dilemmas and double binds. Because women in the United States cannot simultaneously approximate our culturally determined and gender-determined ideal voice prescriptions within the culture, they are presumalby experiencing role conflict, stress and possible rejection.

Carol and Banisa present still another double bind. Women face the paralinguistic double bind.

Carol Ann Valentine and Banisa Saint Damian

COMMUNICATIVE POWER: GENDER AND CULTURE
AS DETERMINANTS OF THE IDEAL VOICE

It is generally believed that gender and culture tend to affect our notions of the "ideal voice," but that these variables are relatively insignificant in comparison to three characteristics of ideal voice typically associated with "good speech": (1) that it be easily understood, (2) unobtrusive, and (3) appropriate (Fisher, 1975). This study explored the universality of widely accepted descriptors of the ideal voice in cross-gender and cross-cultural perspective. The study probed the intersubjective typification of the ideal speaker's voice, the ideal male, and the ideal female voice, in Mexico and the United States. The purpose was to construct and contrast the ideal voice types within and across these two cultures. The research questions which guided the study were: What are the collectively perceived "ideal voice types" in Mexico and the United States? Then, to what degree do the ideal male and ideal female voice types correspond to the ideal voice type within each culture?

Beyond the conceptualization of the notion of the "ideal" voice is the centrality of the concern in contemporary social and political life. "How did I sound?" is an often asked question by those seeking personal or public prominence or response.

Sometimes this question is prompted by a radio or television interview and at other times the question is promoted by self evaluation. Whatever the motivation the question is a lingering and elusive one.

Culturally, in the United States we have some biases about a "good" voice and what it sounds like. As previously stated, Fisher (1975) iterates the dimensions, but do these apply across cultures and across genders?

Specifically, what do research and folk wisdom say about a good voice? Morton Cooper, speech pathologist and author of *Change Your Voice, Change Your Life*, says, "Today's most desirable voice image is 'deep macho' for men and sultry, deep, sexual, the Lauren Bacall voice' for women."

Indeed, are these the collective perceptions of the ideal voice and, if so, are these perceptions culture bound? That is, how do people describe what they

Carol Ann Valentine is an Associate Professor in the Department of Communication, Arizona State University, Tempe, AZ 85287-1205.

Banisa Saint Damian is an Adjunct Professor in the Department of Communication, Arizona State University, Tempe, AZ 85287-1205.

The authors are indebted to Dr. Richard Nagasawa, Department of Sociology for his invaluable contributions to this research.

consider to be a good voice and are these perceptions widely shared by males and females in the United States and Mexico?

Males and females were selected for survey because of the generally obvious physiological difference between the genders and because of recent discussion of the sociological difference. That is, it has been speculated that women's lack of success in the business world can be partially attributed to the "typical" women's voice. The assumption seems to be that the female voice is simply not seen as appropriate for a serious business person.

Mexico was selected as a cultural comparison for several reasons. Proximity and relative ease of data collection was a factor. Spanish language fluency of one author was another. The reality of sampling a different culture was a factor as was an awareness that Hispanics are the fastest growing minority group in the United States. Understanding of the cultural perspective of this group could facilitate acculturation.

Review of the Literature

Studies examining vocal characteristics of males and females, both within the United States and between the culture of the United States and other cultures, have generally explored paralanguage from four principal perspectives. These perspectives could be characterized as (1) measurable differences, (2) cultural stereotypes, (3) interaction of paraverbal and actual language, (4) developmental expectations.

One body of studies has looked at measurable differences between males and females in their respective use of such vocalic features as pitch, intonation and pronunciation. Empirical investigations, for example, of sex-based linguistic differences in voice pitch have established that females typically have higher-pitched voices and males lower-pitched voices due to both anatomical and cultural factors (Carrel & Tiffany, 1960; Duffy, 1970; Snedicor, 1951). Females' intonation patterns (pitch, stress, juncture) employ more variability than male intonation patterns (Ginet, 1974; Richards, 1975; Snedicor, 1940, 1951). Brend (1975) found that the characterization of female intonation as expressive and male intonation as monotonic could be attributed to the consistent use by males of only the three lowest notes on the intonation scale, whereas, females consistently used four. Furthermore, Brend found that, unlike females, "Men avoid final patterns which do not terminate at the lowest level of pitch, and use a final short upstep only for special effects, incomplete sequence, and for certain interrogative sentences" (1975, p. 86).

Empirical examination of measurable sex-based differences in pronunciation have consistently revealed that females are more likely to use linguistic forms characterized by correctness, free of regionalism or slang (Fasold, 1968; Fisher, 1958; Labov, 1966; Trudgill, 1972). From their review of sex differences in language, Thorne and Henley (1975) contend that correctness of female speech is probably the best documented of all sex-based linguistic differences.

A second body of studies focused on the cultural stereotypes of male/female paralanguage, identifying underlying expectations of gender- differentiated use of language. Jespersen (1922) provides an early portrayal of the stereotypes attached to male/female linguistic behavior. Jespersen characterized women's language as refined, euphemistic, and utilizing hyperbolic expressions, while asserting that male language was more innovative and used more slang. Current beliefs and stereotypes generally continue to suggest that women's speech is weaker and less effective than men's (Kramer, 1974).

Traits attributed to male speaking behavior include such things as forceful, blunt, boastful, and traits attributed to female speaking behavior include emotional, detailed, gentle (Kramer, 1975). In addition, researchers have found that the vocal cue used most to discriminate between male/female speech was speech rate. Men are stereotyped as having a more stable speech rate than women (Broverman, Vogel, Broverman, Clarkson & Rosenkrantz, 1972). A third body of studies has examined the interaction between expectations of paraverbal behavior and actual language use in order to measure the process of selective perception perpetuating the cultural stereotypes of paralinguistic gender differences. Since few actual differences in language use have been empirically validated, the persistence of stereotypes suggests that perceivers are attributing more differences to male messages and female messages than are actually present. This interactive effect, resulting in selective perception, is illustrated by a recent study of male and female professors. In this study, males' and females' classroom behavior was judged differentially by student evaluators according to the sex of the professor, even when the professors used the same teaching behavior (Richardson, Macke, & Cook, 1980). Another example of selective perception is the characterization of female speaking as being loud, typically when females are not conforming to stereotypical gender-determined speaking behavior.

The fourth body of studies investigated the prescriptive power of stereotypes on actual sex-role related speech behavior. "If interpersonal expectancies influence social interaction so as to create their own reality, people who are targets of stereotypes may conform to such expectancies and provide confirming behavioral evidence" (Christensen & Rosenthal, 1982, p. 76). The pervasive nature of sex-role stereotypes exerts pressure on individuals to behave in sex-appropriate ways throughout their lives (Broverman, Vogel, Broverman, Clarkson & Rosenkrantz, 1972; Rubble & Higgins, 1976). Sachs, Lieberman and Erickson (1973) found that this process extends to speech communication behavior and begins at an early age. The researchers reported that judges could identify the voices of prepuberty children by sex. Since there were no essential differences in their voice mechanisms, the differences could not be attributed to anatomical sex differences. Sachs (1975) suggests that boys and girls have learned to speak in a voice and speech style appropriate for their sex. Austin (1965) likewise, observed that little boys tend to be nasal and little girls tend to be oral.

None of these four perspectives on differences in male/female linguistic behaviors has attempted to obtain a shared perception within or between cultural groups, of the ideal speaker's voice, or, indeed, the ideal male or ideal female voice. The study addresses this. There might be some data within the previously cited sources that would provide fragmentary information about ideal voice types, but it is inferential in nature. For instance, a handbook for radio announcers (quoted by Key, 1972) stated that the reason women announcers were replaced by men after World War II when men once more become available was that "often the higher-pitched female voices were frequently vehicles for an overly polished, ultrasophisticated delivery that sounded phoney." Is this an indicator of some of the components of the ideal voice, or, is this a presumption of a small group of people (i.e., radio station owners) of what the public considers the ideal voice?

An example of inferred differences across cultures that possibly indicates aspects of the ideal voice further highlights this point. A broadcaster, citing the reason why so few women were employed as reporters by television networks in the United States asserted that "As a whole, people don't like to hear women's voices telling them serious things" (Mannes, 1969). On the other hand, a survey conducted in Munich, Germany in 1983 by the Institute for Applied Psychology found that "catastrophes don't seem nearly as catastrophic when reported by a female broadcaster." The effect was directly attributed by German psychologists to "the more dulcet tones of the female voice." Is this an indirect indicator of cultural differences in the ideal voice between Germans and Americans? Or, could the results be attributed to other variables than the vocal cues cited? It is clear that intersubjective typification of what constitutes the ideal voice, the ideal male voice and the ideal female voice is required to separate out this information that is only indirectly alluded to in prior studies. This study will use intersubjective typification to construct and contrast ideal types in a more direct and systematic manner.

In their typification studies, Berger and Luckmann (1967) suggested that knowledge of a stock of common social actions generally allows individuals to smoothly negotiate the everyday world. Schutz and Luckmann (1973) further developed the concept of a "stock of knowledge" as a compilation of collectively perceived "ideal types" which act as behavioral models in everyday life. McKinney (1969) described the human tendency toward typification or structuring of the world by means of categorical types as a central feature of human cognition.

This study probes the intersubjective typification of the ideal speaker's voice, the ideal male and the ideal female voice in samples of university students in Mexico and the United States. Its purpose is to construct and contrast the ideal voice types cross-culturally. The analysis of these typifications within and between cultures extends our understanding of the structure of the "stock of knowledge" alluded to by Berger, Luckmann, Schutz and other social scientists in the United States.

Further, the purpose is to integrate extant knowledge of the four perspectives of vocal characteristics with data that compress and expand categories and approaches. That is, some dimensions of previous work are considered in different contexts which wrest new information.

Methodology

In order to construct and contrast the ideal, the ideal male, and the ideal female voice typifications in Mexico and the United States, university students of similar socioeconomic backgrounds between the ages of seventeen and twenty-four were asked to complete a two-part survey instrument. Part one of the survey was an open-ended paragraph; part two was a semantic differential response.

In the first part, the subjects were asked to write a paragraph describing the ideal voice type under consideration. The "ideal voice" instrument was administered to 99 student subjects at the Universidad Autonoma de Guadalajara in Mexico and 98 student respondents at Arizona State University in the United States during the 1982-1983 scholastic year. The instrument to determine the "ideal male voice" was completed by 45 students in Mexico and 59 students in the United States, and the "ideal female voice" ratings were completed by 45 students in Mexico and 69 students in the United States during the same time period. Sample subjects were cross-culturally comparable in age and socioeconomic status.

The descriptors used by the subjects to describe the ideal voice types were abstracted through content analysis by a team of bilingual researchers. Table 1 presents the list of descriptors based upon the responses to the directive: Describe the "ideal voice," the "ideal male voice," and the "ideal female voice."

The bilingual research team first listed and counted all descriptors elicited from respondents. After perusal of the entire list in both Spanish and English, there appeared to be a natural break point in the number of times a given descriptor was listed. The decision to include a specific descriptor was determined numerically as follows: any descriptor mentioned four times or more in any of the three ideal voice patterns was included for further consideration. For example, the word "consistent" was used more than four times in the category "ideal voice in the United States." "Consistent" was thus included as a descriptor. The responses were then converted to the percentage of respondents who mentioned a given descriptor in each voice category. For example, Table 1 indicates that the descriptor "clear enunciation"is more important in Mexico than in the United States; i.e., 97 percent of the Mexican respondents mentioned it, in contrast to 52 percent of the United States respondents.

In the second part of the research instrument, the semantic differential technique was employed to ascertain the collective perception of the ideal voice types on the dimensions of pitch, rate, volume and clarity of diction. Four universal vocal descriptor categories were identified for consideration by a cross-cultural panel of faculty members in sociology and communication : (1) pitch, (2) volume, (3) rate, and (4) diction. The corresponding adjective sets--

Table 1

Descriptors Derived from Content Analysis Concerning the Ideal, Ideal Male, and Ideal Female Voice Types in Mexico and the United States

	MEXICO			UNITED STATES		
	Ideal %	Ideal Male %	Ideal Female %	Ideal Ideal %	Ideal Male %	Female %
Clear enunciation *Buena entonacion*	97	80	69	52	48	24
Firm *Firme*	03	33	04	10	25	06
Well-modulated *Bien modulada*	23	16	20	14	07	06
Without regional accent *Sin acento regional*	09	00	00	08	00	00
Delicate *Delicada*	00	00	20	00	00	00
Sensual *Sensual*	00	00	16	03	07	00
Cheerful *Agradable*	17	16	16	11	07	01
Sincere *Sincera*	00	00	00	06	00	04
Consistent *Consistente*	00	00	00	05	03	03
Medium in pitch *Media en timbre*	30	02	27	07	06	19

Table 1, continued

	MEXICO			UNITED STATES		
	Ideal %	Ideal Male %	Ideal Female %	Ideal Ideal %	Ideal Male %	Female %
Somewhat Low *Algo baja*	08	04	04	14	35	15
Low-pitched *Baja*	15	42	04	20	38	06
Loud *Fuerte*	15	60	00	02	00	00
Somewhat loud *Algo fuerte*	12	11	00	04	07	04
Somewhat soft *Algo suave*	02	02	02	04	07	04
Soft *Suave*	00	00	64	05	04	28
Somewhat Rapid *Algo rapida*	14	04	04	04	00	03
Somewhat slow *Algo despacia*	14	16	18	38	09	20
	N=99	N=45	N=45	N=98	N=69	N=69

*Percent is based upon the number of respondents who listed the descriptor.
**For initial analysis, any descriptor listed four times or more was included.
***Samples were drawn from the Universidad Autonoma de Guadalajara and Arizona State University.

high/low, loud/soft, rapid/slow, and careful/relaxed diction--served as the polar ends of the seven point scales. Figure 1 provides a sample of the semantic differential scale instrument.

La voz ideal de un locutor de radio es...
ALTA   .   .   .   . BAJA
FUERTE   .   .   .   .   .   . SUAVE
RAPIDA   .   .   .   .   .   . LENTA
DICCION   .   .   .   .   . .DICCION
CUIDADOSA   .   .   .   .   .   . LAXA

Figure 1

The mean scores of subjects' responses to the polar scales depicted in Figure 1 provided the mean descriptors of the ideal, ideal male, and the ideal female voice types by country presented in Table 2. The mean scores indicate that the ideal male voice is slightly lower in pitch than the ideal speaker's voice, and noticeably lower in pitch than the ideal female voice in both Mexico and the United States.

Table 2

Mean Descriptors of the Ideal, Ideal Male, and Ideal Female Voice in Mexico and the United States

	MEXICO			UNITED STATES		
	Ideal %	Ideal Male %	Ideal Female %	Ideal Ideal %	Ideal Male %	Female %
Pitch: HIGH/LOW	5.2	5.4	5.1	5.4	5.8	4.8
Volume: LOUD/SOFT	4.5	3.3	5.5	4.7	5.0	5.4
Rate: RAPID/SLOW	4.5	4.7	4.8	4.9	5.1	5.2
Diction:CAREFUL/RELAXED	3.0	3.0	3.0	4.4	4.8	4.5
	N=99	N=45	N=45	N=98	N=69	N=69

Data sources included the Universidad Autonoma de Guadalajara in Jalisco, Mexico, and Arizona State University in the United States.

The ideal voice is perceived as medium in volume in both cultures (4.5 in Mexico and 4.7 in the United States) in contrast to the softer volume expectation for the ideal female voice (5.5 in Mexico and 5.4 in the United States). The most noticeable cross-cultural difference in the table involves the ideal male voice which is expected to be considerably louder in Mexico than in the United States. This difference in expectation is evidenced by an average of over two positive points on the semantic scale.

The ideal, ideal male, and ideal female voice types in Mexico and the United States are depicted as extremely close in semantic space with regard to rate. The six ideal voice types vary less than half a point. The most consistent difference cross-culturally occurs in the category of diction in which the three ideal voice types in Mexico are identical (3.0). This is in contrast to the ideal voice types in the United States which are described as considerably less concerned with care in enunciation (4.4 to 4.8).

To effect further analysis, Osgood's D statistic (Osgood et al., 1957) was used to determine the "common meaning assigned to the ideal voice types." This statistic allows the researcher to measure the degree to which groups differ in their use of descriptors of the ideal, ideal male, and ideal female voice types. More specifically, the D statistic measures the distance between two concepts. In this case the concept areas are ideal and the ideal gender-determined voice in common semantic space. These pairs were derived from the responses to the semantic differentials. The formula is:

$$D_{ij} = \overline{(X_i - X_j)^2} = \overline{d_{ij}^2}$$

In this formula, D is the linear distance between concepts of ideal voice i and j, and X_i and X_j are the scores derived for ideal voice types i and

The differences (D's) are computed for all the paired combinations of the concepts and arranged in a symmetrical matrix to find the ideal voice typifications which cluster or "go together."

The use of the D statistic extended the analysis capacity of the study of ideal voice types. That is, through its use it was possible to contrast and compare not only the individual component descriptors of the three ideal voice types within and between cultures, but also the overall conceptual fit of the six constructed types to one another.

Figure 3 portrays the relationships among the ideal voice typifications in the United States. In contrast to the situation in Mexico, the ideal and the ideal male voice types in the United States form a close match: both are described as firm, low, cheerful, well-modulated, somewhat slow in rate of delivery, and characterized by clear enunciation. Since volume was not significantly mentioned in the ideal type, no comparison based upon that characteristic is possible.

FIGURE 3

THE RELATIONSHIPS AMONG THE IDEAL, IDEAL MALE, AND
IDEAL FEMALE VOICE TYPES IN THE UNITED STATES.

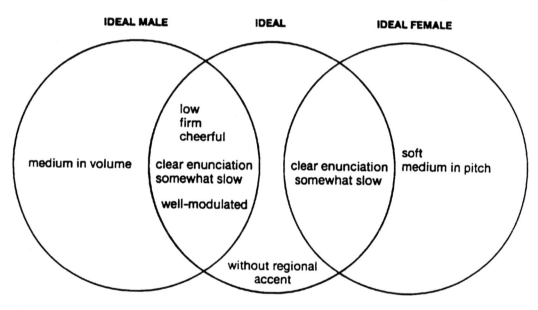

IDEAL MALE   IDEAL   IDEAL FEMALE

low
firm
cheerful

medium in volume   clear enunciation   soft
                     somewhat slow   clear enunciation   medium in pitch
                                        somewhat slow
                     well-modulated

                        without regional
                        accent

* Derived from Tables 3 and 4 of this study based upon samples drawn from the Universidad Autónoma de Guadalajara and Arizona State University.

In contrast to the close match between the "ideal/ideal male" voice pair, the female ideal voice type is identified by two descriptors which preclude simultaneous approximation of the ideal female and the ideal speaker's voice ideals. A female can either conform to the feminine ideal typification by being soft in volume and medium in pitch, or approximate the ideal speaker's voice by speaking with moderate volume and low pitch; adherence to one ideal type precludes close approximation to the other.

Between Country Comparisons

Figures 4, 5, and 6 contrast the ideal voice types between cultures. Figure 4 reveals very close correspondence between the ideal male voice in Mexico and the United States: both are described as firm, low, cheerful, well-modulated, somewhat slow with pauses, and characterized by clear enunciation. In only one dimension do the culturally determined ideal male voice types differ: the Mexican male ideal is depicted as loud whereas the United States ideal male is described as moderate or medium in volume.

FIGURE 4

A COMPARISON OF THE IDEAL MALE VOICE TYPES IN MEXICO AND THE U.S.

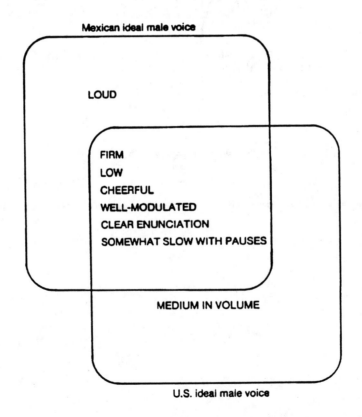

Mexican ideal male voice

LOUD

FIRM
LOW
CHEERFUL
WELL-MODULATED
CLEAR ENUNCIATION
SOMEWHAT SLOW WITH PAUSES

MEDIUM IN VOLUME

U.S. ideal male voice

* Derived from Tables 3 and 4 of this study based upon samples drawn from the Universidad Autónoma de Guadalajara and Arizona State University.

Figure 5 suggests that the ideal female voice type in both Mexico and the United States is soft in volume, clear in enunciation, medium in pitch, and somewhat slow with pauses. However, in addition, the Mexican ideal voice type is depicted as sensual, delicate, and cheerful.

FIGURE 5

A COMPARISON OF THE IDEAL FEMALE VOICE TYPES IN MEXICO AND THE U.S.

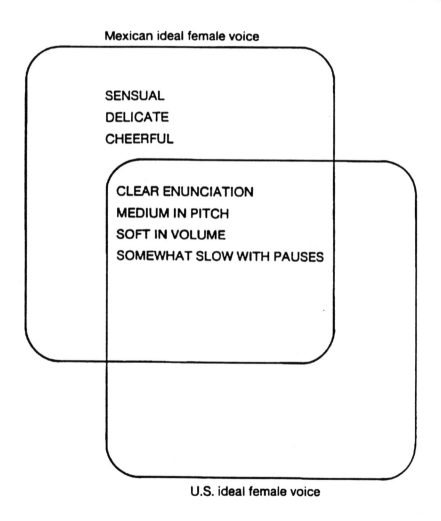

Mexican ideal female voice

SENSUAL

DELICATE

CHEERFUL

CLEAR ENUNCIATION

MEDIUM IN PITCH

SOFT IN VOLUME

SOMEWHAT SLOW WITH PAUSES

U.S. ideal female voice

* Derived from Tables 3 and 4 of this study based upon data drawn from samples in the Universidad Autónoma de Guadalajara and Arizona State University.

Figure 6 portrays the relationship between the ideal speaker's voice across cultures. Both ideal voice types are described as cheerful, well- modulated and characterized by a clear enunciation without regional accent. In contrast to the Mexican ideal voice type which is expected to be medium in rate and pitch, and loud in volume, the United States ideal type is identified as firm, low, and somewhat slow with pauses. Thus the qualities associated with the ideal speaker's voice differ in rate, pitch, and volume in Mexico and the United States.

FIGURE 6
A COMPARISON OF THE IDEAL SPEAKER'S VOICE TYPES IN MEXICO AND THE U.S.

Mexican ideal speaker's voice

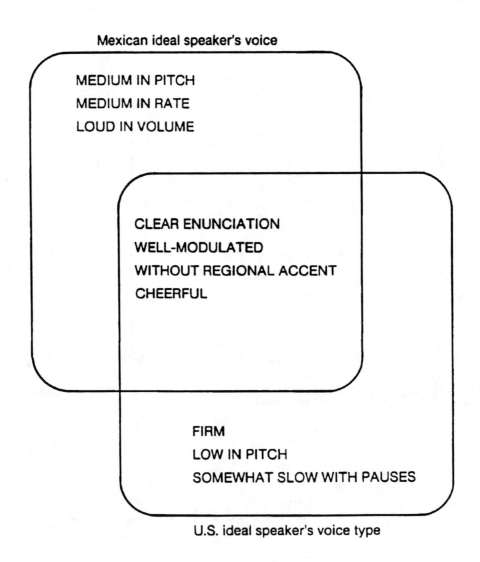

MEDIUM IN PITCH
MEDIUM IN RATE
LOUD IN VOLUME

CLEAR ENUNCIATION
WELL-MODULATED
WITHOUT REGIONAL ACCENT
CHEERFUL

FIRM
LOW IN PITCH
SOMEWHAT SLOW WITH PAUSES

U.S. ideal speaker's voice type

* Derived from Tables 3 and 4 based upon data drawn from the Universidad Autónoma de Guadalajara and Arizona State University.

Osgood's D Matrix

The D matrix analysis or Osgood's D statistic was employed to analyze the ideal, ideal male, and ideal female voice types in terms of the following four basic vocal components:pitch, volume, rate, and care with diction. The D statistic provided an objective measure of the relative location of the ideal voice types in common semantic space. Table 5 presents the matrices that give the distance between the voice types in Mexico and in the United States.

For the Mexican sample, the D's suggest that the ideal female voice is closest to what is considered to be the "ideal voice." Although the male ideal voice is also linked to the "ideal voice," it is not quite as close to the ideal as the female ideal type. The D for the "ideal voice/ideal female voic e" pair shows the lowest value in the matrix (1.05) which suggests that the ideal voice and the ideal female voice are perceived as having a common semantic space. The D for the "ideal voice/ideal male voice" is also relatively low (1.23) suggesting a similar though less marked tendency toward common meaning. In both instances the ideal voice is the voice in common. Unlike the gender ideal/ideal voice pairs, the "ideal male/ideal female" pair does not appear in a common semantic space in Mexico (D = 2.22).

Data Analysis

Descriptors of the ideal voice derived from content analysis are depicted in Tables 3 and 4. These tables include vocal descriptors spontaneously mentioned by more than 7 percent of the subjects surveyed in Mexico and the United States. For example, Table 3 indicates that the adjective "delicate" was elicited from 7 percent or more of the respondents in only one of the categories considered: ideal female voice in Mexico.

Table 4 includes the vocal descriptors concerned with pitch, rate, and volume. The model descriptor in each category was used for contrastive analysis. From this table, it can be detected that the ideal male pitch in both Mexico and the United States is low, and that the ideal female pitch in both countries is medium. Thus, the pitch of the ideal female voice more closely approximates the ideal speaker's voice in Mexico. In contrast, the ideal male voice is most closely associated with the pitch ideal in the United States. Also, the ideal female voice is soft in volume in contrast to both the ideal and the ideal male voice typifications in Mexico and the United States.

Table 3

Mean Descriptors of the Ideal, Ideal Male, and Ideal Female Voice in Mexico and the United States

| | MEXICO | | | UNITED STATES | | |
	Ideal %	Ideal Male %	Ideal Female %	Ideal Ideal %	Ideal Male %	Female %
Clear enunciation	+	+	+	+	+	+
Firm	0	+	0	+	+	0
Well-modulated	+	+	+	+	+	0
Without regional accent	+	0	/	+	0	0
Delicate	0	0	+	0	0	0
Sensual	0	0	+	0	0	0
Cheerful	+	+	+	+	+	0
	N=99	N=45	N=45	N=98	N=69	N=69

+ = mentioned by 7 percent or more of the sample population.
0 = mentioned by less than 7 percent of the sample population.
Samples were drawn from the Universidad Autonoma de Guadalajara and Arizona State University during the 1982-83 scholastic year.

Table 4

Modal Descriptors Derived From Content Analysis of the Ideal, Ideal Male, and Ideal Female Voice Types in Mexico and the U. S.

| | MEXICO | | | UNITED STATES | | |
Descriptor Category	Ideal %	Ideal Male %	Ideal Female %	Ideal Ideal %	Ideal Male %	Female %
Pitch	Medium	Low	Medium	Low	Low	Medium
Volume	Loud	Loud	Soft	Medium	Medium	Soft
Rate	Medium	Some-what slow	Some-what slow	Some-what slow	Some-what slow	Some-what slow

Samples were drawn from the Universidad Autonoma de Guadalajara and Arizona State University during the 1982-83 scholastic year.

Within Country Comparisons

Figure 2 portrays the relationships among the ideal voice types within the Mexican culture. The figure shows that the ideal and the ideal male voice types in Mexico share four qualities in common. Both the ideal and ideal male are loud, cheerful, well-modulated, and characterized by clear enunciation. In contrast to the ideal voice, the ideal male voice is additionally identified as firm, low and somewhat slow in rate of delivery with pauses.

FIGURE 2

THE RELATIONSHIPS AMONG THE IDEAL, IDEAL MALE, AND IDEAL FEMALE VOICE TYPES IN MEXICO.

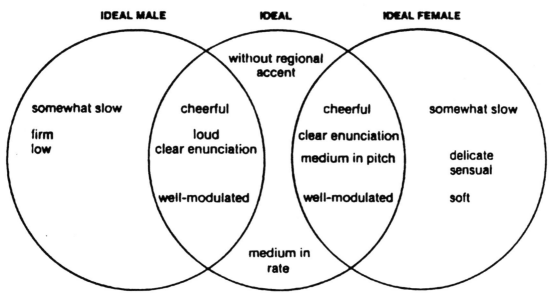

* Derived from Tables 3 and 4 of this study based upon samples drawn from the Universidad Autónoma de Guadalajara and Arizona State University.

The ideal female voice type in Mexico also shares four qualities in common with the ideal voice type: they are both described as cheerful, well-modulated, medium in pitch, and characterized by clear enunciation. In contrast to both the ideal and the ideal male voice types, the female ideal voice type is additionally described as delicate, sensual, and soft.

Hofman's Transformation Matrix

To transform the D matrices, the D's in each matrix are divided by the square root of the summed distances in the matrix. This sums to unity and hence makes the matrices comparable. The transformed D's (labeled D_n) from the pooled matrices now approximate normality. D is expressed as follows:

$$\cdot \, D_n = \frac{D_q}{\sqrt{\sum_{q}^{n} D2}} \qquad \text{and} \qquad \sum^{n} (Dr_{nq}) = 1.0$$

In this transformation formula, D is a transformed D and n is the number of interconcept distances between items in the matrix. The critical distance is determined according to how the concepts cluster in the matrices which constitute the distribution; the small D_n's load some- where below the grand mean so that an upper limit of one interval below the grand mean can be used as the critical distance. The critical distance determined through this transformation is applied to all the matrices of the samples contained in Table 5 of this study in order to determine which concepts go together or have common meaning, and which stand outside common meaning as determined by semantic distance.

It should be noted that the D values are arbitrary in the sense that the D's are relative to each other and not based upon an objective criterion to determine a critical D that defines members of a group or cluster. Thus the question might be raised: How small must a D be relative to other D's in the matrix in order to define them as possessing common semantic space? Hofman (1966) suggests a method whereby a critical distance can be determined so that distances smaller in value will define members as having common meaning, or clustering characteristics. He suggests the transformation of the D matrices to permit the use of normal curve statistics to select a critical distance.

Table 6 represents the D matrices for the two groups. It reveals that the initial analysis presented in Table 5 is correct with one exception: the tentative conclusion concerning the link between the "ideal female/ideal voice" pair in the United States. The critical D value determined through the Hofman transformation ($Dn = .49$) definitely excludes this as a pair of concepts possessing common meaning: the characteristics of the ideal speaker's voice and the ideal female voice do not cluster sufficiently to occupy the same semantic space.

Table 5

D Matrices

| | MEXICO | | | UNITED STATES | | |
	Ideal	Male	Female	Ideal	Male	Female
Ideal	X	1.23	1.05	X	.707	1.01
Male		X	2.22		X	1.12
Female			X		X	

Table 6

D Matrices

| | MEXICO | | | UNITED STATES | | |
	Ideal	Male	Female	Ideal	Male	Female
Ideal	X	.448	.382	X	.423	.605
Male		X	.807		X	.671
Female			X		X	

Statistical value = .49

Data for Tables 5 and 6 derived from Table 2 of this study based upon data drawn from the Universidad Autonoma de Guadalahara and Arizona State University.

Overall voice types comparisons across cultures reveal that the Mexican and the United States ideal voice types differ in one major respect: in Mexico, the ideal female voice type is closer to the ideal voice than the male ideal voice is. In contrast, the United States male ideal voice is closest to the cultural ideal, and the female ideal voice is not related to the ideal speaker's voice.

For the United States sample, the D's in Table 5 suggest that the ideal male voice is closest to the ideal voice in semantic space (D = 707). The female ideal voice is not as close to the ideal voice as its male counterpart (D = 1.01), however it is closer to the ideal speaker's voice than it is to the ideal male voice (D = 1.12). Thus, the male and the female ideal voice types are furthest apart in semantic space in the United States, as in Mexico. However, in contrast to Mexico, the male ideal voice in the United States is closest to the ideal voice type.

SUMMARY OF RESULTS

Intrasocietal Analysis

The ideal, ideal male, and ideal female voice types in Mexico were closely matched on the dimensions of pitch, rate, and care with diction.

The three voice types were characterized as somewhat low-to-medium in pitch, medium in rate of delivery, and careful in enunciation or diction; they differed noticeably in only one dimension: volume. Neither the male nor the female ideal type approximated the medium volume of the ideal speaker's voice type; the male was louder, and the female was softer than the ideal. Descriptors spontaneously elicited to further define the ideal types in Mexico revealed differentiation in which only the female voice was expected to be sensual and delicate, and only the male voice was expected to be firm or authoritarian. Neither gender type in Mexico was identified in terms of descriptors which would allow simultaneous approximation of the ideal cultural voice type.

Intrasocial analysis of the ideal voice types in the United States considering the four dimensions of pitch, volume, rate, and care with diction revealed that, as in Mexico, neither gender type completely conformed to the ideal speaker's voice type, However, the ideal male voice conformed much more closely than the ideal female voice. Thus, a United States male can approach both the ideal and the ideal male voice communi- cation patterns with few conflicting behavioral directives. In contrast, the United States female cannot enact the cultural and gender-determined ideal voice types without experiencing considerable role conflict.

Intersocietal Analysis

A comparison of the ideal speaker's voice type across the cultures of Mexico and the United States revealed that they share the qualities of clear enunciation and cheerfulness, while being well-modulated and free of regional accent. The perception of ideal pitch and rate varied across cultures: The ideal in Mexico was described as medium in pitch and rate while the ideal in the United States was low in pitch and somewhat slow in rate. Additionally, the ideal speaker's voice in Mexico was described as loud and the ideal in the United States was further characterized as firm.

Intrasocietal comparison of the ideal male voice types revealed that the ideal male vocal delivery was somewhat low in pitch and somewhat slow in delivery. Both ideal male voice types were additionally described as firm, cheerful, well-modulated, and careful in enunciation. However, the ideal Mexican male was expected to use greater volume and take more care with diction than his United States counterpart.

The ideal female voice types in Mexico and the United States were similarly described as soft in volume, medium to somewhat slow in rate of delivery, and careful in enunciation. However, the ideal Mexican female voice was additionally expected to sound delicate and sensual.

DISCUSSION

The ideal speaker's voice in both Mexico and the United States did not conform completely to either ideal gender type in the respective country, and the ideal gender types provided the closest cross-cultural match of the paired types considered. This raises some interesting questions. Is there a common denominator in human perception of gender ideal voice types that transcends culture? Why do the United States with its predominantly Anglo Protestant heritage, and Mexico with its Hispanic Catholic heritage share gender-related perceptions of the ideal voice generally assumed to be the product of acculturation? Are these parallel perceptions an approximation of male and female archetypes?

The accentuated differences expressed in both preference and expectation between the ideal male and female voice types in Mexico could be a reflection of the more traditional nature of the society; i.e., the more traditional the culture, the more the actual differences between the sexes would be exaggerated in the socialization process to maintain maximum dimorphism, or social and biological differentiation of the sexes (Van den Berghe, 1973). It would follow that the relatively few actual gender related differences in male/female paralanguage would be accented and exaggerated through the socialization process in a more traditional culture.

The findings of this study in the less traditional culture of the United States further expands this point. No such clear-cut identifiers of traditional femininity such as delicate, sensual, and cheerful were suggested for the ideal female voice in the United States. This difference may be explained by the differing degree of traditionalism in the two cultures. Although the United States is somewhat traditional, it is more industrialized and less homogeneous in political, economic, and religious structure than Mexico in which institutional reinforcement tends to create congruent messages concerning sex role socialization. Thus, the female ideal voice is more clearly and consistently identified with refinement and affective communication generally associated with the traditional female role in Mexico.

In contrast, the pluralistic culture of the United States has generated social and political movements which have eroded the homogeneity of messages emanating from the various cultural institutions concerning sex role socialization and diffused their impact, resulting in multiple and sometimes conflicting behavioral expectations. The data suggest that, in contrast to Mexico, the United States female is faced with a singular dilemma: She cannot enact the cultural and gender-determined ideal voice types without experiencing role conflict. By conforming to the ideal female voice type, she automatically dissociates herself from her culture's ideal voice type.

In this regard, the recent trend to use female television reporters with voices lower in pitch than the average United States female voice raises several questions. With an increasing availability of atypical female role models in the media, is an interactive effect occurring in which the perception of the ideal female voice is converging upon the ideal speaker's voice type in the United States to resolve conflicting directives for females in communication industries?

In summary, the identified differences between the ideal female voice types in this study may reflect the differing degrees of traditionalism present in the two societies, and the evolving United States female ideal voice in broadcasting. Females in the media may be selectively deleting traditionally feminine vocal characteristics in an effort to approximate the ideal and the ideal male voice types in the United States.

REFERENCES

Austin, W.M. (1965). Some social aspects of paralanguage. *Canadian Journal of Linguistics, 11*, 31-39.

Berger, P., & Luckmann, T. (1967). *The Social Construction of Reality*. Garden City, NY: Doubleday and Co.

Brend, R.M. (1975). Male-female intonation patterns in American English. In B. Thorne & N. Henley (Eds.), *Language and sex: Difference and dominance*. Rowley, MA: Newbury Press.

Broverman, I.K., Vogel, S.R., Broverman, D.M., Clarkson, F.E., & Rosenkrantz, P.S. (1972). Sex-role stereotypes: A Current appraisal. *Journal of Social Issues, 28*, 59-78.

Carrel, J., & Tiffany, W. (1960). *Phonetics: Theory and application to speech improvement*. New York: McGraw-Hill.

Christensen, D., & Rosenthal, R. (no date). Gender and nonverbal decoding skill as determinants of interpersonal expectancy effects. *Journal of Personality and Social Psychology, 42*, 75-87.

Duffy, R. (1970). Fundamental frequency characteristics of adolescent females. *Language and Speech, 13*, 14-24.

Fasold, R.W. (1968). A sociological study of the pronunciation of three vowels in Detroit speech. Washington, DC: Center for Applied Linguistics.

Fisher, H.B. (1975). *Improving voice and articulation*. Boston, MA: Houghton Mifflin.

Fisher, J.L. (1958). Social influence on the choice of a linguistic variant. *Word, 14*, 47-56.

Ginet, S.M. (1974). Linguistic behavior and the double standard. Paper presented at the Conference on Intercultural Communication, Binghamton, NY.

Henley, N.M. (1975). Power, sex, and nonverbal communication. In B. Thorne & N. Henley (Eds.), *Language and sex: Difference and dominance.* Rowley, MA: Newbury House.

Hofman, J. (1967). An analysis of concept-clusters in semantic inter-concept space. *American Journal of Psychology, 80,* 345-354.

Jespersen, O.L. (1922). *Language: Its nature, development and origin.* London: Allen and Unwin.

Key, M.R. (1972). Linguistic behavior of male and female. *Linguistics, 88,* 15-31.

Kramer, C. (1974). Folklinguistics. *Psychology Today, 8,* 82-85.

Kramer, C. (1975). Female and male perceptions of female and male speech. Paper presented at the Meeting of the American Sociological Association.

Labov, W. (1966). The social stratification of English in New York City. Washington, DC: Center for Applied Linguistics.

Mannes, M. (1969). Women are equal but --. In J.M. Bachelor, R.L. Henry, & R. Salisbury (Eds.), *Current thinking and writing.* New York: Appleton-Century-Crofts.

McKinney, J.C. (1969). Typifications, typologies, and sociological theory. *Social Forces, 48(1),* 1-11.

Osgood, C.E., Suci, G.I., & Tannenbaum, P.H. (1957). *The measurement of meaning.* Urbana, IL: University of Illinois Press.

Richards, D.M. (1975). A comparative study of the intonation characteristics of young adult males and females. Unpublished doctoral dissertation. Cleveland, OH: Case Western Reserve University.

Richardson, L.W., Cook, J.A., & Macke, A.S. (1981). Classroom authority management of male and female professors.

Richardson, L. *The dynamics of sex and gender.* Boston, MA: Houghton Mifflin Company.

Rubble, D.N., & Higgins, E.T. (1976). Effects of group sex composition on self-presentation and sex-typing. *Journal of Social Issues, 32,* 125-132.

Sachs, J. (1975). Cues to the identification of sex in children's speech. In B. Thorne & N. Henley (Eds.), *Language and sex: Difference and dominance.* Rowley, MA: Newbury House.

Sachs, J., Lieberman, P., & Erickson, D. (1973). Anatomical and cultural determinants of male and female speech. In R.W. Shuy & R.W. Fasold (Eds.), *Language attitudes: Current trends and prospects* (pp. 74-84). Washington, DC: Georgetown University Press.

Schutz, A., & Luckmann, T. (1973). *Structures of the life-world.* Evanston, IL: Northwestern University Press.

Snedicor, J.C. (1940). Studies in the pitch and duration characteristics of superior speakers. Unpublished doctoral dissertation. Ames: State University of Iowa.

Snedicor, J.C. (1951). The pitch and duration characteristics of superior female speakers during oral reading. *Journal of Speech and Hearing Disorders, 61,* 44-52.

Thorne, B. , & N. Henley. (1975). Difference and dominance: An overview of language, gender, and society. In B. Thorne, & N. Henley (Eds.), *Language and sex: Difference and dominance.* Rowley, MA: Newbury House.

Trudgill, P. (1972). Sex, covert prestige, and linguistic change in the urban British English of Norwich. *Language in Society, 1,* 179-195.

BIBLIOGRAPHY

Abercrombie, D. (1966). Paralanguage. *British Journal of Disorders of Communication, 3,* 55-59.

Addington, D.W. (1968). The relationship of selected vocal characteristics to personality perception. *Speech Monographs, 35,* 492-503.

Addington, D.W. (1971). The effect of vocal variations on ratings of source credibility. *Speech Monographs, 38,* 242-247. Allport, G.W. , & Cantril, H. (1934). Judging personality from voice. *Journal of Social Psychology, 5,* 37-54.

Aronovitch, C.D. (1976). The voice of personality: Stereotyped judgments and their relation to voice quality and sex of speaker. *Journal of Social Psychology, 99,* 207-220.

Atmyanandana, V. (1976). An experimental study on the detection of deception in cross-cultural communication. Unpublished paper. Tallahassee: Florida State University.

Austin, W.M. (1965). Some social aspects of paralanguage. *Canadian Journal of Linguistics, 11,* 31-39.

Baird, J.C., & Tice, M. (1969). Imitative modeling of vocal intensity. *Psychonomic Science, 19,* 219-220.

Barnlund, D.C., Kendon, A. , Harris, R.M., & Key, M.R. (1975). Communication styles in two cultures: Japan and the United States. In *Organization of behavior in face-to-face interaction.* The Hague: Mouton.

Bateson, M.C. (1963). Kinesics and paralanguage. *Science,* 139-200.

Battle, L.D. (1963). New dimensions in cultural communication. *Publications of the Modern Language Association, 78(2),* 15-19.

Beebe, S.A. (1976). Effects of eye contact and vocal inflection upon comprehension and credibility. Unpublished doctoral dissertation. Columbia: University of Missouri.

Beekman, S.J. (1973). Sex differences in nonverbal behavior. Unpublished paper. East Lansing: Michigan State University.

Beier, E.G. , & Zautra, A.J. (1972). Identification of vocal communication of emotions across cultures. *Journal of Consulting Clinical Psychology, 39,* 166.

Bentler, P.M., & Lavoie, A.L. (1972). A nonverbal semantic differential. *Journal of Verbal Learning Verbal Behavior, 11(4)*, 491-496.

Berger, P., & Luckmann, T. (1967). *The social construction of reality.* Garden City, NY: Doubleday and Co.

Berryman, C.L., & Eman, V.A. (Eds.). (1980). *Communication, language & sex.* Rowley, MA: Newbury House.

Black, J.W. (1942). A study of voice merit. *Quarterly Journal of Speech, 28,* 67-74.

Blahna, L.J., Eakins, B., Eakins, R., & Lieb-Brilhart, B. (1975). A survey of the research of sex differences in nonverbal communication. In Siscom 1975: *Women's (and men's) communication.* Austin, TX: Proceedings of the Speech Communication Association Summer Conference II.

Bowler, N. (1964). A fundamental frequency analysis of harsh vocal quality. *Speech Monographs, 31,* 128-134.

Bradford, A., Ferror, D., & Bradford, G. (1974). Evaluation reactions of college students to the dialect difference in the English of Mexican-Americans. *Language and Speech, 17,* 255-270.

Brandt, L.J. (1965). Differences among children from two socioeconomic groups in their responses to tone and words in communication. Unpublished masters thesis. Worcester, MA: Clark University.

Brend, R.M. (1975). Male-female intonation patterns in American English. In B. Thorne & N. Henley (Eds.), *Language and sex: Difference and dominance.* Rowley, MA: Newbury Press.

Brown, B.L. (no date). Paralinguistics: The tacit dimension in social interaction. *International Journal of Soc. Language.*

Brown, B.L., Strong, W.J. & Rencher, A.C. (1973). Perceptions of personality from speech: Effects of manipulation on acoustical parameters. *Journal of the Acoustical Society of America, 54,* 29-33.

Brown, B .L., Strong, W.J., & Rencher, A.C. (1974). Fifty-four voices from two: The effects of simultaneous manipulations of rate, mean fundamental frequency and variance of fundamental frequency on ratings of personality from speech. *Journal of the Acoustical Society of America, 55,* 313-318.

Broverman, I.K., Vogel, S.R., Broverman, D.M., Clarkson, F.E., & Rosenkrantz, P.S. (1972). Sex-role stereotypes: A current appraisal. *Journal of Social Issues, 28,* 59-78.

Carrel, J., & Tiffany, W. (1960). *Phonetics: Theory and application to speech improvement.* New York: McGraw-Hill.

Christensen, D., & Rosenthal, R. (no date). Gender and nonverbal decoding skill as determinants of interpersonal expectancy effects. *Journal of Personality and Social Psychology, 42,* 75-87.

Duffy, R. (1970). Fundamental frequency characteristics of adolescent females. *Language and Speech, 13,* 34-24.

Fasold, R.W. (1968). *A sociological Study of the pronunciation of three vowels in Detroit speech.* Washington, DC: Center for Applied Linguistics.

Female broadcasters' voices soften news. (1983, January 9). *Arizona Republic,* p. F-10, cols. 1-2.

Fisher, H.B. (1975). *Improving voice and articulation.* Boston, MA: Houghton Mifflin.

Fisher, J.L. (1958). Social influence on the choice of a linguistic variant. *Word, 14,* 47-56.

Franken, J. (1982). Voices generated by men or women: An effect in the perception of the adequacy of a response. Unpublished paper. Tempe, AZ: Arizona State University, Department of Communication.

Ginet, S.M. (1974). Linguistic behavior and the double standard. Paper presented at the Conference on Intercultural Communication, Binghamton, NY.

Hartford, B. (no date). Phonological differences in the English of adolescent Chicanos and Chicanas. In Dubois and Crouch (pp. 73-80). (Title of book not given, publication site not given).

Henley, N.M. (1975). Power, sex and nonverbal communication. In B. Thorne & N. Henley (Eds.), *Language and sex: Difference and dominance.* Rowley, MA: Newbury House.

Hofman, J. (1967). An analysis of concept-clusters in semantic inter-concept space. *American Journal of Psychology, 80,* 345-354.

Jaspersen, O.L. (1922). *Language: Its nature, development and origin.* London: Allen and Unwin.

Key, M.R. (1972). Linguistic behavior of male and female. *Linguistics, 88,* 15-31.

Kramarae, C. (1981). *Women and men speaking.* Rowley, MA: Newbury House.

Kramer, C. (1974). Folklinguistics. *Psychology Today, 8,* 82-85.

Kramer, C. (1974). Women's speech: Separate but unequal? *Quarterly Journal of Speech, 60,* 14-24.

Kramer, C. (1975). Female and male perceptions of female and male speech. Paper presented at the Meeting of the American Sociological Association (site not given).

Labov, W. (1966). The social stratification of English in New York City. Washington, DC: Center for Applied Linguistics.

Laver, J.D. (1968). Voice quality and indexical information. *British Journal of Disorders of Communication, 33,* 43-54.

Mannes, M. (1969). Women are equal but --. In J.M. Bachelor, R.L. Henry, & R. Salisbury (Eds.), *Current thinking and writing.* New York: Appleton-Century-Crofts.

Martyna, W. (1981). Language and the sexes: A bibliography. Unpublished paper. Santa Cruz, CA: Stevenson College-University of California.

McConnell-Ginet, S. (1978). Intonation in a man's world. *Signs: Journal of Women in Culture and Society, 3(3),* 541-559.

McKinney, J.C. (1966). *Constructive typology and social theory*. New York: Meredith Publishing.

McKinney, J.C. (1969). Typifications, typologies, and sociological theory. *Social Forces, 48(1)*, 1-11.

Osgood, C.E., Suci, G.I., & Tannenbaum, P.H. (1957). *The measurement of meaning*. Urbana: University of Illinois Press.

Richards, D.M. (1975). A comparative study of intonation characteristics of young adult males and females. Unpublished doctoral dissertation. Cleveland, OH: Case Western Reserve University.

Richardson, L.W., Cook, J.A., & Macke, A.S. (1981). Classroom authority management of male and female professors. Mentioned in L.W. Richardson, *The dynamics of sex and gender*. Boston, MA: Houghton Mifflin Company.

Rubble, D.N., & Higgins, E.T. (1976). Effects of group sex composition on self-presentation and sex-typing. *Journal of Social Issues, 32*, 125-132.

Sachs, J. (1975). Cues to the identification of sex in children's speech. In B. Thorne & N. Henley (Eds.), *Language and sex: Difference and dominance*. Rowley, MA: Newbury House.

Sachs, J., Lieberman, P., & Erickson, D. (1973). Anatomical and cultural determinants of male and female speech. In R.W. Shuy & R.W. Fasold (Eds.), *Language attitudes: Current trends and prospects* (pp. 73-84). Washington, DC: Georgetown University Press.

Schutz, A., & Luckmann, T. (1973). Structures of the life-world. Evanston, IL: Northwestern University Press.

Schwartz, M. (1968). Identification of speaker sex from isolated, voice-less fricatives. *Journal of the Acoustical Society of America, 43(5)*, 1178-1179.

Schwartz, M., & Rine, H. (1968). Identification of speaker sex from isolated whispered vowels. *Journal of the Acoustical Society of America, 44(6)*, 1736-1737.

Snedicor, J.C. (1940). Studies in the pitch and duration characteristics of superior speakers. Unpublished doctoral dissertation. Ames: State University of Iowa.

Snedicor, J.C. (1951). The pitch and duration characteristics of superior female speakers during oral reading. *Journal of Speech and Hearing Disorders, 61*, 44-52.

Sprague, J., & Ruhly, S. (1978). Male-female communication differences in the U.S.: Review and cultural analysis of principal literature. Paper presented at the Sixth International Colloquium on Verbal Communication.

Thorne, B., & Henley, N. (1975). Difference and dominance: An overview of language, gender, and society. In B. Thorne & N. Henley (Eds.), *Language and sex: Difference and dominance*. Rowley, MA: Newbury House.

Trudgill, P. (1972). Sex, covert prestige, and linguistic change in the urban British English of Norwich. *Language in Society, 1*, 179-195.

Uris, D. (1975). *A woman's voice: A handbook to successful private and public speaking*. New York: Stein and Day.

Wright, J.T. (1982). Typifications, ideal types and research methodologies. Unpublished paper. Tempe, AZ: Arizona State University.

SYNOPSIS . . . . .

Barbara Taynton Crawford draws conclusions about women and their communicative power based on a fascinating review of her personal professional experience superimposed on the literature. Armed with humility and real experiences that convinced her she would never make it as a "good ol' boy," Crawford's paper records her ten conclusions about the connections and the strategies.

Much of Crawford's paper harkens back to Hoar's and Sayer's papers. Context is critical. Men and women need to learn the impact of context and can benefit from learning about the wide variety of available communication strategies. In concluding, Crawford pleads for increased research on successful and, by implication, unsuccessful female communication behaviors.

Crawford does not and did not intend to provide a history of how we got in the circumstance. Many of us, however, have a suspicion that our graduate schools have long had an impact. Some watchwords were "never mind about comparing males and females, you'll just confound the data."

Check the assumptions here. If assumed, they will lead you to inexorable conclusions that many of us find frighteningly real. Don't read this one just before sleeping. You might well have similar bad dreams or is the term "nightmares" closer to the truth?

Barbara Taynton Crawford

WOMEN AND COMMUNICATIVE POWER: A CONCEPTUAL APPROACH TO COMMUNICATION STRATEGIES

This paper is based on certain assumptions and theoretical positions: (1) power is an important variable in communication; (2) all persons have power (3) meaning is contextual; (4) women and men are socialized to use communicative power in different ways; (5) male communicative strengths are more valued in the contexts where power brokering takes place; (6) in a democratic culture, power "ought" to be equally distributed (one person; one vote); (7) sexual stereotypes in the use of power are reinforced by "self" and "other;" (8) women are double-binded over the issue of whether to use male communicative strengths and thus risk alienating their "audience," or whether to use "effective" strategies which may perpetuate the status quo; (9) one method of resolving this apparent conflict is to approach communicative power as being contextually determined; and so (10) to develop courses in Communication in which men and, especially, women are taught a variety of ways of using power. People also need to be taught to analyze the context in order to develop strategies which are effective in both the long and short term. This last assumption is sometimes called the androgynous communicator position. However, the contextual analysis must take into accoudt the sex of the communicators because females are seen as being less effective in many contexts.

After I was out of graduate school for two years, my idealism about effectively winning arguments with men by the use of logical argumentation was shattered. It happened when, as Vice-President of the Faculty Senate, I was automatically made a member of the prestigious inner circle called "The Council." At the second meeting of the group, the President had introduced an idea and had asked for feedback. There was a pause as he looked about with his eyebrows raised expectantly, and I took a breath and prepared to speak. I wanted to give him important information about some possible impacts of the ideas he had just presented. I was trained in Group Discussion and Organizational Communication courses, and I taught Business Speech classes at the time, so I was sure that feedback from the lower ranks of the organization was vital to the success of the outcome. At that point, I was interrupted by one of the good old boys who said sardonically to the group, "We all know what you think, Barbara!" which was followed by uproarious laughter. That was the first clue . . .

Barbara Taynton Crawford is an Associate Professor in the Department of Communication, Santa Barbara City College, Santa Barbara, California.

I learned that though I might be "well spoken," I could never be "a good man." "So I shut up, fumed, and decided to "get smarter." With variations on this theme, my experience is repeated many times a day in board rooms, classrooms, factories, and homes. Some of the positions I have come to many years after that event are stated in the first paragraphs of this paper. I reached these hypotheses through reading, research, and classroom teaching. I'd like to explain parts of this process to you for feedback and discussion.

1. **Power is an Important Variable in Communication**

Power can be defined as the ability to accomplish X, and let X equal anything the person can desire. Because we live in a culture which values "doing" as opposed to "being," according to our colleagues in Intercultural Communication, we believe "accomplishing" as the end product of "doing" is important and value it positively. When people get together to "do" things, if there is a disagreement about "what" to do, those persons with the most salient power get done that which they think needs to be done. For the purposes of this paper let us define salient power as being that power which is currently effective in the context. Potential power is all the kinds of power, other than salient, possibly available in the context.

2. **All Persons Have Power**

Those with the potential power may feel powerless and respond by: (a) doing what others think needs doing ("going along" with) and taking pride in the group's accomplishment; (b) pretending to "go along" and use nondirect means of accomplishinga different goal (subverting the goal), or (c) rebel and refuse to cooperate (destroy the group effort to accomplish a particular goal). Therefore, power becomes a most important variable in contexts where there is disagreement on what to do. In case one, those with salient power can be assured of success; in the other two cases the probability becomes more "iffy," Because those with potential power have the ability to subvert or destroy the accomplishment of those with salient power, it becomes clear that all persons have power, if any one person recognizes this choice in any given context.

3. **Meaning is Contextual**

Because meaning is contextual, many persons don't recognize power if it is potential. Consequently, those who don't realize this power may see themselves or others as being powerless. They are socialized to believe that only some people "should" or "do" have power and that some kinds are "bad" or "evil" so they do not desire or value that particular kind of power. Thus, power is thought to be unequally distributed because of the meanings it has for groups and individuals.

Among the beliefs in our culture which lead to this situation are: "My self interest is defined by what society tells me is best;" "It is wrong, sinful and improper to be self-concerned;" "If there is a winner, everyone else is a loser;" "The only way to behave is according to the rules;" "The use of power always means coercion;" and "Power always corrupts." When persons act as though these beliefs are true, then a dichotomous situation evolves where power vacuums are filled by those who will fill them. These ideas become self-fulfilling prophecies; that is, some persons are thought to be powerful while others are powerless. This is not to deny the fact of unequal distribution of power, only to explain the process that maintains it.

4. Women and Men are Socialized to Use Communicative Power in Different Ways

Women and men are socialized to deploy their power in different ways. The power equation for men is something like this:

$$Power = Brains \times Money$$

while the power equation for women is like this:

$$Power = Looks \times Brains$$

So men are socialized from the cradle on to believe they should learn about the physical world, study hard, assert themselves, be mechanically inclined, be a winner, be entrepreneurial, not cling to sentiment and feeling. A young male grows up believing that his fate is up to him and assertion and brains will bring him money with which he can secure a mate and those physical objects he desires. On the other hand, a young woman is taught to believe that good looks and good manners, when used wisely, will get her a mate who will get her what she needs from the world. The traditional, Cinderella/Prince Charming myth is not dead but seems to be very much alive, at least among my students. Prince Charming as a role model is statistically less desirable to the young male than is Cinderella to his counterpart. Because of this difference in the socialization process, both men and women are taught to deny or undervalue personal strengths that remain only potential for power brokerage. For men, this undervaluing takes place in the general area of the power to nurture altruistically. The undervalued domain for women is generally in the power to assert and direct as well as to be analytical.

5. Male Communicative Strengths are More Valued in the Contexts Where Power Brokerage Takes Place

The main consequence (possibly antecedent) of this socialization process is that the powers men are encouraged to develop are also those powers most valued by the culture in those contexts where power brokerage takes place. Those powers women are encouraged to develop are either time-specific (as in beauty or procreation), limited to a small audience (as in family), or personspecific (as in husband). Please note also that these contexts are transient and subject to the whims and vagaries of the power needs of others. That is, beauty is in the eye of the beholder; children, if one can have them, tend to grow up; and spouses can and do wander or stray. On the other hand, money is a more tractable, traceable, and dependable form of power, as is education, technological information, and a career with status and money.

If women use more of their power to nurture than do men, it is no surprise nor is it particularly unrealistic. Marilyn Monroe couldn't have been all wrong when she sang "Diamonds Are a Girl's Best Friend." Women who deploy their power in this manner are conforming to deeply held cultural values about money and power. "It ' s as easy to fall in love with a rich man as a poor one" is a saying still on the lips of many mothers and daughters. Men are still the power brokers in places where it counts--the larger arena where lots of money and lots of people are impacted by the decisions of a few. The board rooms of banks, corporations, and large public utilities, as well as the "President's Council" in universities are still peopled for the most part by males. The single female or two sprinkled in the mix are largely for looks and for perpetuating the myth that society, like the government, is democratic.

6. We Believe That in a Democratic Culture Power Should Be Equally Distributed

One of the reasons that "power brokers" do sprinkle "powerplaces" with women is we as a culture believe that with a "one man, one vote" kind of democracy women "ought" to be proportionally represented in the workplace. As a result of believing two unreconcilable ideas, we are confused. On the one hand, many deeply believe in the democratic principle and experience guilt if they recognize inequality in tangibles like pay, rank, and opportunities. Some of those same people also believe that women should be pleasant and easy to be with, not rivals. To many men and women the power used by women should be representative of the person's sexual orientation to be valid and accepted as legitimate. This belief is communicated in such sayings as "Honey is better than vinegar," "She knows how to get something done with the bat of an eye;" and "She can smooth over ruffled feathers"--which may be, by intent, compliments on conflict resolution skills. Their consequence is frequently quite different.

7. Sexual Stereotypes are Reinforced by "Self" and "Other"

When is a compliment not a compliment? When it functions as a reinforcer for negative behaviors, there is no compliment. Sexual stereotypes, as with all stereotypes, don't simply wither and die like "old soldiers," even with goodwill and good intentions. Because men and women are conflicted about how women ought to deploy their powers, we tend to reinforce in others the behaviors we find comfortable, reliable and predictable. Simple little social reinforcers, like strokes to Pavlov's dog, tend to perpetuate behaviors, especially comfortable, reliable, and predictable behaviors like sex role stereotypes. Thus, women smile when complimented on cooking or clothing or "smoothing ruffled feelings," and men become self-satisfied over a compliment on "winning" a contract, "beating" an opponent, etc. I am amazed at gatherings of professional women how much social time is taken up with these reinforcers. I can recall seeing the director of an outreach college--a well known and published author--fall into the little girl behavior of blushing and demurly saying, "Oh, do you really think so?" when complimented on her cooking by another professional woman who was also a powerful "mover and shaker." Men and women perpetuate sex role stereotypes when we reinforce stereotypical behaviors with compliments. When we reply, genuinely of course, with a positive feedback to these reinforcers, then we also participate in the social self-fulfilling prophecy. In the workplace and classroom they are an anathema to positive change toward a more equal evaluation of performance when actually using salient power. The status quo is thus perpetuated.

8. Women Are "Double-Binded" Over the Issue of Whether to Use Male Communicative Strengths and Thereby Risk Alienating the "Audience," or Whether to Use "Effective Strategies Which May Perpetuate the Status Quo.

Successful women are frequently double-binded over the issue of whether to use "male" communicative strengths and win a battle, but lose the war. Women are often successful in using power, but the after-the- fact attribution is negatively distorted if the person evaluating its use is disconcerted by role behavior which breaks stereotypes. As an example, think of the boss who upon hearing that Miss Jones was very successful in getting a contract replies, "Yes, but she used unladylike language." She is alienating her "audience," though successfully winning contracts. If she decides to switch to "more effective" audience analysis and behavior, she may well perpetuate the status quo. She is thus in the classical Batesonian double-bind. Former Chief Justice of California, Rose Bird, is a case in point. She has been attacked for being too unattractive but is also criticized in the Los Angeles Times of October 8, 1985 by John Balzer while trying to correct that impression, "The Bird... had just completely redone her hair and makeup to make herself more attractive, and had distributed glamorous Holly-wood-style photographs to the media to emphasize this new look." The acceptance of a simple androgynous position toward the teaching of communication skills will not suffice, because women who use male models of successful communication are at risk of loss of effectiveness in the long term.

9. One Way to Resolve This Apparent Conflict is to Approach Communicative Power as Being Contextually Determined

One way to avoid this double-bind situation is to use a contextual approach to understanding communication and power. The context determines what power is salient and what power is only potential. Part of that context is the sex of the communicators.

10. We Need to Develop Courses in Communication Which Teach Students to Analyze Context

Teaching students to analyze the context and develop effective long and short term communication strategies would seem to be most helpful to females and males, too. Men and, especially, women need to learn more about the wide variety of potential power available to them. Then practice building the skills at applying various kinds of power in various contexts could be coached by the hopefully androgynous instructor. I am currently collecting data on what kinds of power men and women think they "ought" to deploy in various contexts, by use of a questionnaire called "The Strength Deployment Inventory," based on Eric Fromm's Man for Himself, no pun intended. As a first step to clarifying some basic human patterns in this and other cultures, I think it may be useful in discovering what is "expected" gender communication behavior. What is necessary to successful model building for developing contextual strategies is more research into "successful" female communication behaviors in which the context is included as part of the analysis. We need to aid people in experiencing a wide variety of their potential powers.

SYNOPSIS . . . . .

Several of the preceding papers considered the effects of gender stereotyping, women's lack of perceived power, and the muting of women's voices. These themes converge in Suzanne Condray's examination of the media strategies used by the National Organization of Women and its attempt to attract support for the Equal Rights Amendment. Condray's paper is the study of the search for power, the power to be heard and the power to influence.

After twenty plus years of NOW we have some rather sophisticated understandings of what worked and what did not work. Condray provides new ammunition. Is the ERA capable of reincarnation?

Her analysis of NOW's efforts shows that the quest for such power is punctuated with barriers: lack of established paths of access, lack of expertise and of funds, and lack of cultural support for female participation in politics. The power sought by NOW proved difficult to achieve in full. NOW strategies were able to overcome the tradition of the muted female voice: they were able to speak, they did achieve the power to be heard. What kept them from influencing their audience was their lack of power, both perceived and actual, within the political and media establishment, as well as the stubborn effects of gender stereotyping. NOW strategists did not have the power to control the way their message was presented, and so they were heard in someone else's context. Because of gender stereotyping, their message was interpreted in ways that were not necessarily productive or influential.

Condray's insightful case history and analysis of NOW's efforts is applicable to other groups that have not had the power to be heard within their own contexts, groups that have not had the power to express themselves as they would choose. On a positive note, NOW's partial success suggests that subsequent efforts could be productive in gaining greater control over NOW's (and other's) context of self-expression.

Suzanne E. Condray

NOW'S MEDIA STRATEGIES AND THE FEMINIZATION OF POWER

The relationship between communication and power is a web intricately woven. In the realm of public policy, communication begets power. Thus, it is no mistake that those voices silenced within the political arena are those which become subjugate and powerless in that area.

Achieving power may take a variety of forms, according to Wrong (1979). These forms include coercion, authority, manipulation, and persuasion. Jaquette (1984), in analyzing Wrong's classification of power, characterizes manipulation and persuasion as forms more readily available and attributable to women, while she characterizes coercion that women do not have access generally to institutions which operate under the auspices of coercion or inducement. Furthermore, she suggests that women are disenfranchised as a group because they are perceived as lacking the credibility to enforce or command legitimate control or status. The theorist argues that women may practice manipulative forms of power out of a frustration for their socially-imposed powerlessness. Similarly, women may adopt persuasive techniques in an attempt to influence the public sphere. However, as Jaquette argues, persuasion is not a reliable resource necessarily in that "persuasion requires access to information, the capacity to know and to attack the status quo through the formulation of new ideology" (1984, p. 19-20). Persuasion becomes then a diminuitive form of power dependent upon the practice of reason, and the effective practice of reason becomes dependent upon an access to and application of rhetorical strategies.

Within the contemporary political environment, groups desiring to influence public policy often have used the media as a means to persuade public opinion and affect policymaking and thus achieve power (Gitlin, 1980). The National Organization for Women (NOW) represents such an organization which chose certain media tactics as a means to attract support for the Equal Rights Amendment. This study analyzes the media strategies NOW adopted during the ERA ratification campaign as NOW sought to persuade those within the public and political sphere to support the amendment.

NOW's lack of direct access to the political spectrum posed an obstacle for the organization in lobbying for the ERA. Such an obstacle was not new to those women seeking political recognition. Dahlerup (1984, p. 34) describes these obstacles as typical of the biases of many Western liberal democracies, when she

Suzanne E. Condray is Associate Professor and Chair of the Speech Communication Department at Denison University in Granville, Ohio 43023.

writes, "Not only do large groups of people never participate in the political process, but issues are also systematically excluded from serious consideration by the political systems." Dahlerup characterizes these omissions within the political process as the structural exclusion of specific groups or issues. Among these excluded, according to Dahlerup, are women and their concerns. The structural bias is one marked in two ways -- first, by the nature of the institution, and second, by the ability of women to penetrate the structure of that institution.

With the passage of the Nineteenth Amendment, women gained a legal franchise to participate in the political arena by means of casting votes. Nevertheless, proponents of equal rights for women continued to face numerous obstacles, from 1923, when they introduced the measure to Congress, through the struggle for state ratification in the 1970s and the 1980s (Berry, 1986). Countless barriers existed and still remain, to women's active participation in the political system. NOW, as many women's organizations, confronted not only an institution opposed in many ways to the ERA, but one exhibiting negative cultural attitudes towards women's participation in politics. As McGlen and O'Connor (1983) acknowledge, these and other societal norms prevented women from not only becoming involved in politics but in acquiring the skills required for political activity. In addition to these barriers, women lacked the financial resources to fund effective political campaigns. Bachrach and Baratz (1970) recognize these barriers as symtomatic of a structural suppression related to the socialization of women and the long period through which women have been unable to quesiton patriarchal order. Dahlerup (1984), in explaining Bachrach and Baratz' hypothesis, suggests:

> The fact that certain resources are necessary to one to become a political representative means that exactly those who have an interest in challenging the existing distribution of resources do not have the opportunity to be elected in great numbers. And the system or corporate interest-representation within the state administration does . . . make strong barriers for the interests that are not integrated into this system.

These types of barriers made it necessary for NOW to assess and adopt persuasive strategies which provided alternative means to achieve political power. NOW had to determine how best to gain public recognition of the Equal Rights Amendment and its status within the political process. In an attempt to further its goals, NOW chose to take its message of equlaity direclty to the public via the mass media. Between 1970 and 1982, NOW adopted media strategies as a means of raising public consciousness and support for the amendment. These strategies became instrumental in the organization's attempt to build a national coalition and establish a political agenda.

In some cases, these media strategies preempted the discussion of ERA as evolving from the political arena and created a public forum through which proponents and opponents debated the amendment. In other cases, the media provided a means to publicize debates within the political spectrum. The former provided NOW an opportunity to gain recognition of its own campagin while the latter, presented NOW an opportunity in which to draw public attention to those individuals and constituencies in the political institution who belittled or threatened gender equality. In addition, the organization adopted media strategies which recognized the number of ERA supporters who hertofore had been ignored largely by the press. The tactics also offered the organization the public exposure necessary to increase the number of supporters. Morris (1974, p. 528) recognizes the strategies as prudent in building support for such social movements as those promoting women's rights. Says Morris, "presumably if members of the general public, in seeing and discussing items of news from the communications media, become participants in, rather than observers of, events, such persons would then become members of a special public," one notably capable and perhaps willing to act in promoting movement concerns. This action would create a potential movement for growth in the number of supporters but perhaps even for the media's recognition of the legitimacy of the campaign.

NOW confronted a couple of problems, however, in its initial attempts to design effective media strategies. First, the media served as an institution which disenfranchised women. Women neither occupied major decision-making roles within the media, nor did they represent a group which gained much coverage by the institution (Gans, 1979). NOW had to determine whether to choose an alternative means of obtaining or creating its own press coverage or to cultivate supporters among those in the media profession. Secondly, in its infancy, NOW lacked recognition as a "spokesparty" for the various constituencies of women, even though it identified itself as a national organization representing the concerns of women. Of that problem, Freeman (1975, p. 80) writes:

> As the only action organization concerned with women's rights, it had attracted many different kinds of people with many different views on what and how to proceed. With only a national structure and at this point no base, it was difficult for individuals to pursue their particular concerns on a local level; they had to persuade the whole organization to support them.

Throughout the early days of NOW, there seemed to be a reluctance on the part of women in the country to "adopt a collective consciousness" in lobbying for women's equality. Costain (1982) argues that many women, as others unaccustomed to maneuvering in the political mainstream, perceived these tactics as unorthodox and threatening. In order for NOW to establish itself as a legitimate

Suzanne E. Condray

NOW'S MEDIA STRATEGIES AND THE FEMINIZATION OF POWER

The relationship between communication and power is a web intricately woven. In the realm of public policy, communication begets power. Thus, it is no mistake that those voices silenced within the political arena are those which become subjugate and powerless in that area.

Achieving power may take a variety of forms, according to Wrong (1979). These forms include coercion, authority, manipulation, and persuasion. Jaquette (1984), in analyzing Wrong's classification of power, characterizes manipulation and persuasion as forms more readily available and attributable to women, while she characterizes coercion that women do not have access generally to institutions which operate under the auspices of coercion or inducement. Furthermore, she suggests that women are disenfranchised as a group because they are perceived as lacking the credibility to enforce or command legitimate control or status. The theorist argues that women may practice manipulative forms of power out of a frustration for their socially-imposed powerlessness. Similarly, women may adopt persuasive techniques in an attempt to influence the public sphere. However, as Jaquette argues, persuasion is not a reliable resource necessarily in that "persuasion requires access to information, the capacity to know and to attack the status quo through the formulation of new ideology" (1984, p. 19-20). Persuasion becomes then a diminuitive form of power dependent upon the practice of reason, and the effective practice of reason becomes dependent upon an access to and application of rhetorical strategies.

Within the contemporary political environment, groups desiring to influence public policy often have used the media as a means to persuade public opinion and affect policymaking and thus achieve power (Gitlin, 1980). The National Organization for Women (NOW) represents such an organization which chose certain media tactics as a means to attract support for the Equal Rights Amendment. This study analyzes the media strategies NOW adopted during the ERA ratification campaign as NOW sought to persuade those within the public and political sphere to support the amendment.

NOW's lack of direct access to the political spectrum posed an obstacle for the organization in lobbying for the ERA. Such an obstacle was not new to those women seeking political recognition. Dahlerup (1984, p. 34) describes these obstacles as typical of the biases of many Western liberal democracies, when she

Suzanne E. Condray is Associate Professor and Chair of the Speech Communication Department at Denison University in Granville, Ohio 43023.

SYNOPSIS.....

Several of the preceding papers considered the effects of gender stereotyping, women's lack of perceived power, and the muting of women's voices. These themes converge in Suzanne Condray's examination of the media strategies used by the National Organization of Women and its attempt to attract support for the Equal Rights Amendment. Condray's paper is the study of the search for power, the power to be heard and the power to influence.

After twenty plus years of NOW we have some rather sophisticated understandings of what worked and what did not work. Condray provides new ammunition. Is the ERA capable of reincarnation?

Her analysis of NOW's efforts shows that the quest for such power is punctuated with barriers: lack of established paths of access, lack of expertise and of funds, and lack of cultural support for female participation in politics. The power sought by NOW proved difficult to achieve in full. NOW strategies were able to overcome the tradition of the muted female voice: they were able to speak, they did achieve the power to be heard. What kept them from influencing their audience was their lack of power, both perceived and actual, within the political and media establishment, as well as the stubborn effects of gender stereotyping. NOW strategists did not have the power to control the way their message was presented, and so they were heard in someone else's context. Because of gender stereotyping, their message was interpreted in ways that were not necessarily productive or influential.

Condray's insightful case history and analysis of NOW's efforts is applicable to other groups that have not had the power to be heard within their own contexts, groups that have not had the power to express themselves as they would choose. On a positive note, NOW's partial success suggests that subsequent efforts could be productive in gaining greater control over NOW's (and other's) context of self-expression.

power representing women, it had to confront and overcome this internal strife and move from an informally-constituted group to an organized coalition. NOW was but one of several women's organizations involved in coalition politics (Joyner, 1982). In building a foundation for a contigency which news organizations recognized as a legitimate institution, and hence offered coverage of that institution, Tuchman (1978) contends that such a progression was necessary. NOW, therefore, had to incorporate these concerns into its media campaign for the ERA.

NOW's Strategies

In designing its media campaign, NOW elected three major courses of action. First, NOW attempted to penetrate institutional barriers informally by establishing media contacts with those believed to be sympathetic to organizational concerns and, formally, by using regulatory measures to evaluate and then amend, where necessary, broadcast coverage of women's issues. Second, organizational representatives designed particular strategies to influence media agenda-setting and coverage to increase public awareness and support of the ERA. Third, NOW adopted measures which usurped mainstream media coverage and presented alternative forms of messages through advertising campaigns and feminist journalism. NOW believed that collectively these tactics could promote a communication environment more conducive than the present for gathering public support. Through these efforts the organization seemed to think it could achieve greater power for women within the public and political spheres.

The miniscule number of women directors, editors, and managers offered NOW little opportunity to influence media decision-making directly. Therefore, NOW chose to develop strategies within the mainstream of the existing regulatory framework to influence managers to uphold non-discriminatory policies and maintain programming standards. The actions served not only ot purge media institutions of discriminatory practices but offered NOW supporters opportunities to participate in collective action.

NOW encouraged television viewers within local chapters to monitor media coverage of women and women's issues in local programming. Where violations of public interest standards occurred, NOW took formal action. For example, under the leadership of a national NOW task force, the Detroit chapter petitioned WXYZ-TV, a local ABC owned and operated station, alleging discriminatory practices in employment and violations of community interest and fairness standards (NOW, PIO, September 1973). Detroit NOW settled with WXYZ-TV when the station agreed to make improvements in its employment of women and in its programming directed at feminist issues and goals. The station also agreed to take under advisement the criticisms of the Women's Advisory Council, a group organized specifically for analyzing programming adhering to the interests of women within the market area. Such actions allowed NOW to utilize existing measures to force compliance. These strategies provided an opportunity to involve local NOW women in media campaign efforts and offered important options for enlisting those women who were uncomfortable supporting less orthodox tactics.

NOW also proposed changes in the National Assocation of Broadcasters' (NAB) Television Code in regard to special programming which "misrepresents, ridicules, or attacks any individual or group on basis of race, sex, creed, color, national origin, or age" (NOW, PIO, October, 1973). While compliance to the NAB Television Code was voluntary, NOW argued that any voluntary compliance to such programming standards generally reflected a station's commitment ot quality programming and public service.

In addition to these actions, NOW utilized affirmative action guidelines as indirect tools in promoting the commercial responsibility of corporations accused of demeaning women in advertising. In the November 1971 Board Meeting, NOW members decided "to explore with Xerox, soap companies, [and] cosmetic companies, etc. . . . the [possibilities of corporate] funding of programs . . . [on the women's movement], in lieu of offensive advertising . . . and as a part of their affirmative action in the public interest" (NOW, Board Meeting, November, 1971). Each of these measures constituted ones which used existing regulatory standards on affirmative action, broadcast access, or governmental employment guidelines. They were used to change women's access to media employment and representation in media.

NOW adopted other strategies within the institutional constructs to attempt to influence media coverage of the ERA. Organizational strategists employed networking tactics in which they identified and then maintained direct contact with individuals who might affect media decision-making. For example, the press office recognized the need to work with individuals like New York **Today Show** producer, Cynthia Samuel, who NOW strategists described as a "solid feminist and an astute political observer" and as one who is often responsible for preparing stories on women's issues for hosts Jane Pauley and Tom Brokaw (NOW, Press List, 1981). NOW then developed lists of press personnel, like Samuels, within major television and publication markets. Those lists provided ready access to contacts on major newspaper staffs, within television network headquarters, and throughout press agencies that migh be sympathetic to organizational concerns.

In addition to maintaining these general contacts, NOW press office personnel composed lists of select reporters and columnists invited to informal interviews with the organization's president. NOW strategists kept notes on each reporter's views, prior coverage of the women's movement, and likely future assignments. These notes were then used in preparing for informal meetings. On occasion, media liaisons contacted news and talk show personnel directly to suggest programming on the ERA. For example, NOW Public Information

Director Dian Terry wrote Barbara Walters commending her for her coverage of women's issues and suggesting upcoming events which she might cover (NOW, PIO, January, 1974). Occasionally, NOW worked in cooperation with reporters assigned to provide national coverage or programming on the women's movement, as was the case in May 1970, when ABC correspondent Marlene Sanders hosted the program "Women's Liberation" (Sanders Papers, 1970).

These tactics allowed NOW to penetrate some of the existing barriers to media access. By establishing communication ties with those already in the media, NOW believed it might influence agenda setting on women's issues. By networking among those reporters and columnists responsive to NOW concerns, the organization hoped to maximize the potential for favorable amendment coverage.

If NOW was going to persuade those within the public sphere that the Equal Rights Amendment is prudent and necessary, the organization believed it had to develop a systematic means of getting press attention and of using that airtime or column space to increase public awareness of and support for the amendment. These goals meant developing organizational strategies for gaining media access and then designing campaigns which would yield the most positive coverage of the amendment. A major obstacle confronting NOW strategists was the difficulty of translating the "issue" of equality into appropriate media rhetoric. [Tuchman (1978) describes issues as "based in analytic explanations of the everyday world as a socially experienced structure," whereas she notes, newswork finds its source in practical activity.] Thus, if NOW wanted to use the media to present the message of ERA, the organization had to develop strategies converting the "issue of equality" into measures most likely to invite periodic attention by news personnel.

NOW adopted five major strategies which reflected the needs of daily news flow. NOW's Public Information Office initiated steps to form a NOW News Service "to provide news of women's issues to suburban and weekly newspapers, radio, and television, with special emphasis on the ERA" (NOW, PIO, 1973). The service, as approved by board members in July 1973, concentrated on media within twenty states where the ERA had not yet been ratified. The goals of the service included supplying ERA news to small city and rural areas not served by the major media, establishing supportive climates for the formation of new local organizational chapters, and providing materials specifically to public broadcasting outlets. In the fall of 1973, NOW's Public Information Office supplemented the goals of the NOW News Service by designing and distributing memos to local chapters on "How to Deal with Press on Controversial Issues," and "How to Promote Chapter Officers as Speakers for Local Clubs and Associations" (NOW, PIO, November 1973). These actions targetted problems of local media access and the needs of NOW chapters in regard to their local media outlets.

Other NOW strategists targeted national press operations. In an attempt to increase the number of articles on ERA in mass circulated magazines, NOW proposed that certain organizational members write or solicit articles bylined by NOW representatives. These articles addressed such issues as The ERA and Working Women, What the ERA Means to Men, The Relationship Between the ERA and the Military Draft, and The Impact of the ERA on the Family (NOW, PIO, November 1973).

Perhaps among NOW's most well-known tactics were those associated with staging events, particularly marches, lobbying efforts, and rallies. In **Making News**, Tuchman (1978) discusses the significance of such events as activities structured in terms of discrete units of time and characterized by the elements of traditional news leads. NOW press personnel took meticulous measures to reconcile planning with press needs. For example, NOW media liaisons wrote detailed memos outlining press scheduling and location requirements to maximize coverage when staging events (NOW, Board Meeting, August, 1974). coordinating national activities for a march on August 26, 1974, NOW press offices printed information packets explaining scheduling deadlines for newspaper, evening television newscast, and weekly national magazine coverage. Packets also detailed procedures for contacting press representatives, conducting press conferences, and positioning camera and microphones for various events. Informational packets on marches included specifications for busing participants, constructing banners, and maintaining crowd controls. It seems to this writer that organizational representatives took extraordinary measures to insure optimal press coverage of ERA-related events.

During the last years of the ratification process, NOW adopted strategies which paralled even more closely those campaigns which attracted major coverage in the national media. Among such tactics included the use of celebrities to endorse movement concerns. For example, NOW scheduled ERA Countdown Rallies in which Alan Alda, Mike Farrell, Marlo Thomas, and Beatrice Arthur, along with others, endorsed the ERA (NOW, ERA Countdown, 1981). By delegating celebrities to specific rallies throughout the country, NOW press personnel attempted to maximize coverage on both national and local media. By including males as well as females among endorsers, the organization hoped to show that support for the ERA crossed gender lines.

Throughout the ratification process, NOW media liaisons and public information officers planned their efforts to obtain both national and local press coverage. By adapting media strategies to publication deadlines, visual events, and other structural, stylistic, and journalistic characteristics, NOW attempted to attract press attention to the organization's agenda for women's rights. While media liaisons faced major obstacles in translating the "issue" of women's equality into the mecca of daily news "events," they undertook endeavors which sought to raise conscousness and direct national attention to the ERA, both significant goals for penetrating first the public sphere and then the political arena.

NOW adopted a third strategy which employed media tactics but did not yield control of the presentation to national and local news services. Instead, the organization relied on advertising campaigns and feminist journalism as means of presenting the issue of equal rights. NOW established its own organizational publications such as **DO IT NOW** and developed its own audio-visual materials, including a slide program entitled "The Beginnings of a Long and Real Revolution" (NOW, PIO, November, 1973). While these publications and resources offered NOW a controlled and favorable environment in which to present its support for the ERA, it did not offer the organization the means to reach a large constituency as did other sources. Also, those exposed to feminist journalism were generally already ERA proponents. The publications served NOW interests in building coalitions but did little to reach the uninformed or apathetic. During the latter part of the ratification period, NOW invested organizational resources in national and local advertising campaigns. NOW employed the services of a Miami advertising firm, Beber Silverstein & Partners Advertising, Inc., to design promotional materials (NOW, Beber Silverstein, 1981). The agency offered full market testing, campaign planning, and media buying services. Although the prospect of advertising represented an expensive endeavor for the organization, it also bolted NOW into a sophisticated media campaign typical of those in the political arena of the 1970s and 1980s. Such measures allowed NOW to compete with heavily funded ERA opponents for direct access to mass audiences. They also allowed NOW to bypass traditional mass communication sources.

Together, these strategies allowed NOW to utilize more effectively certain tools of the media and increase the potential for media access. By monitoring broadcasting station performance and filing complaints where necessary, NOW demonstrated its ability to organize women who were able to take action against media outlets within the context of the existing regulatory framework. Such tactics suggested that though NOW might not have direct access to programming decision-making, its membership could influence that decision-making. In a similar vein, while NOW might not have direct access to decision-makers NOW could network among ERA proponents within the media to encourage coverage of the amendment and organizational actions in that regard. These strategies created the means by which NOW could gain access to an institution otherwise generally unavailable to groups of women. The tactics, however, did not gain the same access that perhaps other groups in the political arena might have. This liability was in part due to the fact that those media personnel among which NOW networed were not always in positions to influence decisions about news content.

By developing news services and promoting organizational members to byline news and feature stories on ERA, NOW offered sources of information to institutions with voracious appetites for material. While these measures provided opportunities for NOW to influence media agenda-setting, they did not guarantee that the press received would be adequate, accurate, or favorable in regards to the organization or to the amendment. For example, recent studies by Hagerty (1982), Sarasohn (1982), Walter (1983), Becker (1984), East and Jurney (1984), and Nicholson (1985) indicate the **New York Times, Chicago Tribune, Los Angeles Times, Boston Globe,** and **Washington Post** provided little if any coverage of the text of the amendment. McCash (1985) discovered tha the news weeklies, **Time, Newsweek,** and **U.S. News,** averaged fewer than two ERA articles per magazine per year. Between 1970 and 1973, no national television network presented the text of the ERA in any newscasts, and between 1973 and the end of the ratification process networks presented miniscule coverage of the text (Condray, 1985). Viewers and readers alike were largely left ignorant of the text of the proposed amendment. This problem played havoc for NOW as suggested by research which indicates that even in the last days of the ratification process a number of individuals had no knowledge of what the amendment stated (Walter, 1983). For example, Zezulin (1982) found in her canvassing of Utah that many people who expressed their disdain for the amendment were astonished when someone told them what the amendment actually stated. At the same time however, an increasing number of Americans indicated they supported equal rights for women. A Gallup Poll (**Gallup Report**, 1981) taken in July 1981 found that 63 percent of those who had heard or read about ERA favored the amendment. These research findings suggest that NOW may have needed to focus more attention on getting coverage of the ERA text.

NOW translated the equal rights issue into rhetoric appropriate for the structures of media messages. By organizing marches and rallies, proponenets presented opportunities for visual coverage. By involving celebrities in organizational activities, strategists encouraged media coverage of the event or activity. The goals of such efforts, nevertheless, did not always reconcile with the interpretation of those efforts by either the media or the public. One could not equate staging an event with defining that event, choosing spokespersons with portraying spokespersons effectively, or organizing and mobilizing supporters with controlling how those supporters would be portrayed in the press. Despite NOW's diligent efforts, it did not have, in many instances, the ability to control media interpretations of their tactics. For example, after spending much effort in preparations for a National ERA March in Washington on July 9, 1978, in which 225 delegations demonstrated support for the ERA extension, NOW's efforts received coverage on only one network news program, ABC News, that evening. In the newscast, ABC gave more attention to a group of 50 Nazi demonstrators than it did to the approximately 100,000 ERA supporters (Condray, 1985). Such coverage did little to further NOW's media efforts and may have evoked more negative than positive coverage of the organization.

NOW's media tactics were also not without criticism from those within the women's movement and from those within the organization. In examining the failure of ratification efforts in Illinois, Mansbridge (1986) contends that while national NOW leaders supported state-wide tactics, such as rallies and demonstations, which would hopefully generate national media coverage, state NOW leaders argued that such tactics would not persuade Illinois legislators to vote in behalf of ERA and such tactics might, in fact, be counter-productive in negatively influencing state support. Pleck (1986) similarly argues that the organization needed to target unratified states. Says Boles (1982 p. 576), "There is an extraordinarily weak linkage between a commerical run on national television during prime time and the vote of a Florida legislator." NOW's critics argued that the organization needed to adopt tactics which might have a more direct effect on ratification than on public awareness and support. The criticisms seem to underline the problems NOW faced in waging its war for ratification on both a national and state level and of adapting the organization's strategies to appropriate media audiences.

Alternative media, such as **DO IT NOW** and other feminist publications, assumed audiences which were traditionally ERA supporters. While such sources could be used to build morale and support among proponents, these sources did little to persuade opposing parties. Advertising and commercial messages designed and released during the Countdown Campaign were in a much better position to influence public opinion. Given the cost of the advertising campaign and the campaign's appearance virtually in the last months of the ratification process, it was not a strategy that NOW used extensively. Thus, it is difficult to measure its effectiveness as a media strategy. Nevertheless, Mayo and Fry (1986) conclude that the lack of money and political and communication expertise among proponents left ERA supporters unable to adapt to the modern media as their predecessors had during the suffrage movement.

In its strategizing, NOW demonstrated its ability to identify and respond to certain institutional barriers presented by the media. NOW also demonstrated that it could use a variety of media tactics in addressing and influencing a mass public. Nonetheless, as Jaquette (1984) argues, the persuasive techniques chosen did not guarantee institutional power nor promise favorable coverage of the organization or of the amendment.

Further research needs to explore the web of inconsistencies in organizational efforts and media portrayals. This study only begins to examine this phenomenon in regard to its significance for women's lives. The form of power chosen and exercised by NOW in its lobbying for the Equal Rights Amendment invites greater analysis as well. The study suggests a need for scholars to evaluate the nature of persuasive strategies adopted by women in the face of institutional barriers. The study also recognizes a need for an analysis of NOW's techniques in context of the organization's ability to control elements of delivery. What this study demonstrates is that critics must begin to determine how organized groups of women can best utilize media as a means of accessing and influencing the public and political arena given those institutional barriers. Such scholarship is prudent to a better understanding of the relationship between communication and power as it affects women.

REFERENCES

Bachrach, P. & Baratz, M. (1970). *Power and poverty*. New York: Oxford University Press.

Becker, D. (1984, January/February). Research project on ERA, Women's Institute for the Press. *Media report to women*, 9-10.

Berry, M.F. (1986). *Why ERA failed: Politics, women's rights, and the amending process of the Constitution*. Bloomington: Indiana University Press.

Boles, J.K. (1982, Fall). Building support for the ERA: A case of 'too much too late.' *Political Science*, 15.

Condray, S.E. (1985, August). *Media coverage of the Equal Rights Amendment*. Unpublished research, Denison University.

Costain, A.N. (1982). Representing women: The transition from social movement to interest gorup. In E. Boneparth (Ed.), *Women, power and policy*. New York: Pergamon Press, Inc.

Dahlerup, D. (1984). Overcoming the barriers: An approach to the study of how women's issues are kept from the political agenda. In J.H. Stiehm (Ed.), *Women's views of the political world of men*. Dobbs Ferry, NY: Transnational Publishers, Inc.

East, C. & Jurney, D.M. (1984, January/February). New directions for news. *Media report to women*, 1, 6-8.

Freeman, J. (1975). *The politics of women's liberation*. New York: Longman.

Gans, H. (1979). *Deciding what's news*. New York: Pantheon.

Gitlin, T. (1980). *The whole world is watching*. Berkeley, CA: University of California Press.

Hagerty, S.C. (1982, July/August). An analysis of the *Chicago Tribune's* coverage of the Equal Rights Amendment: 1977-1981. *Media report to women*, 1, 4-7.

Jaquette, J.S. (1984). Power as ideology: A feminist analysis. In J.H. Stiehm (Ed.), *Women's views of the political world of men*. Dobbs Ferry, NY: Transnational Publishers, Inc.

Joyner, N.D. (1982, Spring/Summer). Coalition politics: A case study of an organization's approach to a single issue. *Women and politics*, 57-70.

Mayo, E., & Fry, J.K. (1986). ERA: Postmortem of a failure in political communication. In J. Hoff-Wilson (Ed.), *Rights of passage: The past and future of the ERA*. Bloomington: Indiana University Press.

McCash, V. (1985, March/April). Only once in 11 years did news magazines quote full text (58 words) in their ERA stories. *Media report to women*, 7-9.

McGlen, N.E., & O'Connor, K. (1983). *Women's rights: The struggle for equality in the nineteenth and twentieth centuries*. New York: Praeger Publishers.

Morris, M.B. (1974). The public definition of a social movement: Women's liberation. *Sociology and social research, 57,* 526-43.

Nicholson, C. (1985, March/April). *Boston Globe* did not report basic facts about ERA. *Media report to women,* 9.

NOW (National Organization for Women). Private papers, Schlesinger Library, Radcliffe College, Boston:

Beber Silverstein & Partners Advertising, Inc., August 1981 (National Office, Folder 16).

ERA countdown rally, June 30, 1981 (National Office, Folder 318).

National ERA march, July 9, 1978 (National Office, Folder 313).

NOW board meeting, August 26, 1974 (National Office, Board Minutes, 1969-July 1975, Folder 12).

NOW board meeting, November 1971 (National Office, Board Minutes, 1969-1975, Box 1).

Press files (National Office, Box 53, Folder 327).

Public Information Office chronological file 1972-1976, Quarterly Status Report (National Office, Box 4).

Public Information Office chronological file, October 1-15, 1973 (National Office, Correspondence Public Information Office, 1973-1974, Box 4).

Public Information Office chronologicl file, September 1973 (National Office, Correspondence of Public Information Office 1973-1974, Folder 4).

Public Information Office, November 1973 status report (National Office, Correspondence of Public Information 1972-1976, Folder 1).

Pleck, E. (1986). Failed strategies; Renewed hope. In J. Hoff-Wilson (Ed.), *Rights of passage: The past and future of the ERA.* Bloomington: Indiana University Press.

Public support for ERA reaches new high. (1981, July). *Gallup report, 190,* 23-25.

Sanders, M. (1970). *Marlene Sanders' papers,* Schlesinger Library, Radcliffe College, Boston.

Sarasohn, L. (1982, September). Research project on ERA, Women's Institute for Freedom of the Press. *Media report to women, 1,* 4-7.

Tuchman, G. (1978). *Making news: A study in the construction of reality.* New York: The Free Press.

Walter, J. (1983, September/October). Research project on ERA, Women's Institute for Freedom of the Press. *Media report to women, 1,* 6.

Wrong, D. (1979). *Power: Its forms, bases and uses.* New York: Harper and Row.

Zezulin, L.S. (1982, May). Canvasser sees myths believed if national media don't tell actual 23 words of ERA. *Media report to women,* 1.

SYNOPSIS . . . . .

Valerie Endress explores alternative conceptions of the communicative power of women as it is related to public address, rhetorical theory, and criticism. Some of the problems that Condray explored in her analytic case history of NOW's attempts to communicate are among the problems explored by Endress as she examines the differences between traditional male rhetoric and traditional female rhetoric.

As a result of her examination of the relationship between feminist scholarship and communicative theory, Endress, like other authors in this collection, calls for an enlarged frame of reference, in this case a broader conceptualization of what constitutes effective rhetoric. She notes the importance of dialogue as well as of debate, of exploration and analysis as well as of influence and control. She extends this call for a more inclusive approach to all of communication research and advocates a greater variety and flexibility in methodologies. As Endress concludes, "it will inevitably alter the ways in which questions are asked and evidence is gathered in future rhetorical and communication research."

Valerie A. Endress

FEMINIST THEORY AND THE CONCEPT OF POWER IN PUBLIC ADDRESS

Much of what is written in current communication research does not adequately address or reflect a full understanding of alternative conceptions of the communicative power of women. We find, for example, that traditional approaches to the subject tend to reward aggressive-cooptive patterns of interaction and devalue interactive-cooperative patterns often associated with women's communication. Because such a style works to lessen the impact of women's patterns of communication, we know that our conceptual frameworks are faulty. Yet, we do not know whether an androgynous style (the creation of a third style) would put both males and females at a disadvantage, or whether a female style of interaction should be endorsed.

Only in the last ten years have a limited number of studies in the discipline detected differences in interaction styles between genders. We can conclude from many of those study that to "speak like a woman" includes not only sex differences, but also involves the relationship between difference and dominance and between gender and power. Those same studies also tell us that "speaking like a woman" is valued less in our society than is "speaking like a man." Moreover, the same speech behavior performed by a woman or by a man will be valued differently. and a strategy when spoken by a woman tends to be systematically devalued.

We must ask ourselves to what extent the models of speaking that we research and teach are male models (assertive, monologistic, dominant), and to what extent do our theoretical constructs based on a male model foster male-centered meanings? Admittedly, we speak, read, and write from a gender-marked place in a particular social and cultural context. By doing so, we are performing political acts which may reveal or conceal the relationship between gender and power. If we move from an evaluative structure, one that without question endorses male-centered meanings, to the exploration of alternative structures, we may then be able to understand the concept of communicative power based on a female experience.

References to women in the academic study of politics tend to stress the degree to which females conform or deviate from the political behavior of males. Studies highlighting the rhetorical behavior of women in the political arena maintain that any differences detected in female performance of political roles

Valerie A. Endress is an Assistant Professor of Communication at Stonehill College, North Easton, MA 02357.

is attributed to the general problem of tokenism rather than any specific gender-related difference. This scholarship is based upon rigid definitions of power and authority in communicative interactions as well as the assumption that the contemporary political system imposes certain attitudes and behaviors that will prove more important than any difference based on sex.

Feminist scholars have long questioned the desirability and practicality of the maintenance of such a system, though, and provide proof to the contrary. Feminist theory offers an alternative hypothesis that critiques the present model by focusing attention on nontraditional patterns of authority through the study of the communication dynamics of associations outside the sphere of public life and formal political behavior as has been defined conventionally. On these grounds, it is possible to predict that as we increase our understanding of the nature of women as audience in the political arena, the so-called gender gap phenomenon will emerge as a major constraint on the patriarchally-rooted policy.

While awareness of women's interest in politics has increased dramatically since the "discovery" of the gender gap in 1980, public knowledge of women's relationship to political power and participation is still based largely on speculation and myth. The origin of these myths might well be traced to the very roots of the American political tradition. As a matter of example, it is the same tradition that is marked by the ostracism of Anne Hutchinson for "stepping out of place" in her struggle for religious and political freedom, as well as the execution of women in the Salem trials following the church fathers' proud declaration that the act represented a "symbolic choking of all women" (Sinclair, 1965, p. 24). It was also the same seventeenth century tradition that declared women were the rightful property of their husbands and guaranteed to fill their lives with subordination and duplicity as the popular wisdom dictated that women remain "saints in the church, angels in the streets, devils in the kitchen, and apes in bed" (Rowbotham, 1972, p. 19).

Rhetorical scholarship, and particularly the study of political communication, is by necessity an intellectually integrative endeavor. History and criticism, based on the epistemic function and nature of rhetoric, must assume a dependent, interconnected and collaborative relationship. Such a consideration should provide a means to evaluate, for example, symbolic interaction, rhetorical constraints and the mythic structure of rhetoric as it discloses power relationships, influences perceptions and promotes rhetorical action. Seldom, however, have historical or rhetorical scholars considered an alternative view of reality, embracing feminist notions of political and rhetorical context. Women have remained virtually among the anonymous in what research has catalogued as "major" political movements. What is considered significant in the course of history often does not include the activities of women. Subsequently, women viewed as an active audience to political rhetoric have seldom merited serious consideration (Keohane, 1981, p. 130).

In terms of these conceptual problems, we are faced with the enormous task of reevaluating the relationship between language and power. We must understand that the traditional view of language as an instrument of domination is shaped by patriarchal values. As Jean Bethke Elshtain points out in her essay on feminist discourse, women, since antiquity, have been barred from politics and afforded no public arena to give them voice. Women's speech, according to traditional notions, amounts to little more than "uninformed," "chaotic" and "reactive noise," devoid of meaning and significance (Elshtain, 1981, p. 130).

While men exclusively inhabited the public forum of symposia and dialectic, women, through their enforced isolation, developed alternative rhetorical forms to suit their private sphere (Elshtain, 1981, p. 129; Spender, 1985, pp. 80-81, 125-133). Instead, its power was more subtle, as women explored the possibilities of using speech as a vehicle for self-analysis and social clarity rather than social control. If public speaking is accepted as the primary forum for political communication and women have been without a space or place to participate in that forum, it is little wonder that we have experienced a research gap in the study of women's political rhetoric.

Equally important conceptual questions must be raised over (1) what subject matter actually constitutes politics, and (2) what are the acceptable forms of political behavior. The appropriate topics for political discussion are determined almost exclusively by males. In other words, the great tradition of political philosophy has been "devised by men, for men and about men" (Sapiro, 1981, pp. 701-702). Given this simple fact, we must first ask ourselves if we have overlooked important and relevant issues and topics brought about by women's talk that may have a bearing on redefining women's political culture and tradition.

Second, if we can define a new topic for political discussion, we must then search for the corresponding locations for that talk. Rhetorical scholars would then have to expand their research beyond traditional sources assigned to political rhetoric. As historians Anne Scott and William Chage noted, the ability of women to structure institutions as an acceptable framework for public activity has been one of the "best kept secrets in American history" (1980, p. 10). The examination of what has been termed a "female subculture" (Scott and Chafe, 1980, p. 10) may well provide important resources for information on the nature and importance of women's activities outside the boundaries of the male-centered political arena.

Rhetorical critics of women's political communication must begin to reevaluate the appropriateness and adequacy of their research tools. Thus far, few studies have considered with any depth the problem of the "generic masculine" in evaluating political rhetoric. And, even fewer studies have considered the nature and function of women as audience to rhetorical discourse.[1] When critics talk about political rhetoric, they generally do so in terms of the rhetor's strategic behavior -- whether it be confrontational or coercive, attributed to motive or fantasy.[2] Although a few promising studies have examined the philosophical and ideological basis of women's rhetoric,3 we have yet to see women's rhetoric evaluated outside the standard forms of male-centered meanings in culture and society. For example, would the rhetoric of the women's movement take on a new meaning if it was not compared to the traditional standards of rhetoric set by the patriarchal institution, but was compared to that body of literature extant on the nature and function of women's talk?4 Or, as a possibility, can we examine women's rhetoric without the inevitable comparison to men's rhetoric and discover its nature and function as a separate rhetorical form? Thus, if we consider the possibilities of the importance of women as a distinct audience to political communication, we would then have to move toward a reevaluation of our methods normally used to understand the nature of the beliefs, attitudes and values of that audience.5

Because feminist scholars are engaged in the dual role of documenting theories and advocating practice, they are caught in the dilemma, according to Eisenstein, of "living simultaneously **in** and **against** the society as it exists" (author's emphasis, 1984, p. 251). At issue is the general question of whether feminist theory should advocate a movement toward insertion into our past and present, or whether it should demand a radical reconceptualization of the traditional notions of culture and society. Whether feminists seek to confront the system for the purpose of change, or choose to redefine their role within the system, they are in agreement that we must find new methods for linking the particulars of women's lives, activities and goals to political consciousness.

From a discussion of the conceptual considerations, several problems associated with the assessment of women's communicative power within a political context emerge: (1) political issues and agendas; (2) depoliticizing of women's issues; (3) domination of patriarchal assumptions in the relationship between history and rhetoric; (4) conceptions of rhetoric based on dominance and control; (5) concept of audience based on dominance and control; (6) methodology based on patriarchal assumptions; and, (7) the relationship between language and divergent views of social power. The seven outlined problems highlight the implied rhetorical constraints and serve as a basis for recommendations directed toward the construction of a feminist model of communication.

The Problem of Political Issues and Agendas

We would have to first direct our attention toward the question of what constitutes a "legitimate" political issue. Because we know that women are required to participate in a male-constructed social and political system, we can assume that traditional issues will dominate in the rhetorical context. Issues such as the political economy, international relations, war and peace, and domestic political dissent will maintain a primary focus in our political rhetoric. We can, however, alter the way in which we approach these issues by considering alternative perspectives based on women's experience. For example, concerning economic issues, we have already begun to address the ways in which changes in public policy have affected women as a group through the development of the concept of the "feminization of poverty." With each issue, the rhetorical critic should consider how the rhetor's message impacts women as a separate and distinct rhetorical audience, rather than assuming an audience of the whole. Such a move would, in essence, legitimate women's experience in a rhetorical context.

The Problem of De-politicizing Women's Issues

We will have to expand our notions about what constitutes a "legitimate" political issue by opening our consideration to topics previously delegated to women's private sphere. The issues of childbearing and motherhood, and the previously untouchable moral issues such as birth control and abortion should be addressed outside the realm of intimate and interpersonal communication and should be politicized to the point that the issues at last constitute legitimate political and rhetorical concerns. They would, therefore, be transformed into an object of critical inquiry.

The Problem of Patriarchal Assumptions in History and Rhetoric

On a much broader basis, we should reevaluate our assumptions about the nature of the relationship between rhetoric and ideology, and between rhetoric and history. We should no longer assume that documented history will provide us with the social, political, and philosophical realities apart from the rhetor's world view. And likewise, we should no longer trust the epistemic function of rhetoric as it impacts the writing of history. We must assume that both rhetoric and history reveal symbolic systems in direct conflict to a feminist perspective. Thus, we are faced with the task of reordering our social reality to include an alternative perspective.

The Problem of Conceptions of Rhetoric Based on Dominance and Control

We should look to alternative rhetorical contexts outside the male domain as a source for political communication. In doing so, we move away from the traditional patterns inherent in the political and rhetorical hierarchy. For example, we might look to consciousness-raising groups as opposed to public debate as a form of communication worthy of serious rhetorical study. We might also look to the rhetoric of single-sex informal and private institutions as evidence of a female subculture. Through the examination of alternative forms, we will eventually face the question of what actually constitutes accurate criteria for "effective" rhetoric. Our present rhetorical standards are based on the patriarchal assumptions rooted in power and social control for the measure of rhetorical success. Understandably, such questions will place our entire rhetorical tradition of American political behavior under scrutiny because if, in fact, we do attempt a "womanization of rhetoric" (emphasizing dialogue rather than debate) how do we accommodate such a change? How does this change affect rules governing discourse? And of special importance to the critic, how does this alter theory and criticism?

The Problem of Conceptions of Audience Based on Dominance and Control

We need to reevaluate our assumptions about audience response to political rhetoric. We have yet to determine in what specific ways gender impacts the assessment of such a variable. We must also determine in what ways the factors of race and class impact this response. And, we need to investigate the extent to which patriarchal expectations of audience response influence both women's actual act of audiencing and the rhetorical critic's judgment in assessing response.

The Problem of Methodology Based on Patriarchal Assumptions

In determining the correct method of analysis for the evaluation of rhetoric, we must consider the role and importance of the use of unconventional artifacts such as oral histories, diaries, and journal entries. And, we must be cautious in our use of methodologies based upon patriarchal principles. For example, fantasy theme analysis is based on the chaining of fantasies originating from a male-controlled social reality. Much of social movement analysis is based upon a concept of strategy, confrontation, and coercion. How are the methods used in the analysis of political communication altered when we consider a feminist perspective of communication?

The Problem of Relationship Between Language and Power

If we accept the notion that language embodies women's oppression, then we must consider language structure and content within the context of political communication. As rhetorical scholars, we must draw upon the rich body of feminist literature that attempts to deal with this issue. We must understand how language has been used as a vehicle for dominance and control. We must also attempt to understand how a feminist definition of the power of language acts to counter traditional perspectives.

The preceding recommendations are designed to direct attention toward an analysis of rhetoric reflective of women's experience. Given the immense controversy surrounding the importance of the gender gap phenomena on American political behavior, it would seem especially fitting that scholars of rhetorical theory and criticism now begin to fill a "research gap" in the investigation of the impact of women's experience on political communication. Both American and European feminist scholars, involved in a complex and interdisciplinary endeavor, have succeeded in bringing into question how research principles and the truths constructed by research reflect a bias toward male-centered meanings, and subsequently, the frameworks and methods aimed at the construction, deconstruction and reconstruction of the notion of a female experience and perception of reality. At issue are the knowledge and symbol systems upon which research is based. Thus, the examination of feminist theory in relation to the concept of women and their communicative power should (1) describe female and male communication from a feminist perspective; (2) reflect the masculinist structures embedded in communication and rhetorical theory and practice; (3) create new metaphors, methods, models and meanings challenging the traditional perspective; and as a result, (4) develop new theoretical and aesthetic frameworks for the enhancement of research. Although feminist scholarship is a mix of several orientations and often differs in the scope of change sought, it will inevitably alter the ways in which questions are asked and evidence is gathered in future rhetorical and communication research.

NOTES

[1] Here, I am referring specifically to communication scholars. My conclusion is confirmed in Foss and Foss as well as Spitzack and Carter.

[2] See for example, Simons, Andrews, Fisher, Bormann.

[3] See Campbell as an example.

[4] See studies found in Thorne, Kramarae and Henley.

[5] Rosaldo makes the point that women have a long history as an audience for political rhetoric and she states ". . . I know of no case where men are required to serve as an obligatory audience to female ritual in political performance" (1980, p. 395).

REFERENCES

Andrews, J.R. (1970). The rhetoric of coercion and persuasion: The Reform Bill of 1832. *The Quarterly Journal of Speech*, *56*, 187-195.

Bormann, E.G. (1972). Fantasy and rhetorical vision: The rhetorical criticism of social reality. *The Quarterly Journal of Speech*, *58*, 396-407.

Campbell, K.K. (1980). The "Solitude of Self": A rationale for feminism. *The Quarterly Journal of Speech*, *66*, 304-312.

SYNOPSIS.....

Beverly Romberger's investigation of how women learn about power in male-female relationships is an excellent example of the kind of variety and flexibility that Fran Sayers advocates. Romberger eschewed the traditional, neat, quantitiative approach, and chose instead the less controlled but far richer method of the oral history. Rather than producing a statistically significant list of the five or six (or however many) most prevalent sources of information, Romberger has given us not only the sources of information but has also shown us how women feel about these sources and about the information itself.

Romberger acknowledges that her findings are not, as they stand, generalizable; however, she suggests that from her findings, one could construct a questionnaire that would yield results that could be generalized. Her work underscores the belief that before we undertake the statistical abstraction of a quantitiative study, we should do some exploration to see what the abstractions might be.

Beverly V. Romberger

"IT'S UP TO THE GIRL TO SAY NO!" COMMONPLACES WOMEN LEARNED ABOUT POWER IN RELATIONSHIPS WITH MEN

And there was that day when the enquiring young man came to see Sandy because of her strange book of psychology. "The Transfiguration of the Commonplace," which had brought so many visitors ....

> "What were the main influences of your school days, Sister Helena? Were they literary or political or personal? Was it Calvinism?
> Sandy said: "There was a Miss Jean Brodie in her prime."

Anyone familiar with Muriel Spark's *The Prime of Miss Jean Brodie* cannot help but recognize the significant impact Miss Brodie's words--her conversation, maxims, and narrations--had upon the development of her five adolescent pupils at the Marica Blaine School for Girls. The cultural and social reality of "being female" emerges powerfully in this novel from the talk that takes place between Miss Brodie and the "Brodie set."

The reference in the narration to Sandy's "strange book of psychology, "The Transfiguration of the Commonplace"" relates directly to this study. Muriel Spark transformed the familiar ideas, words and phrases of Miss Jean Brodie. She transfigures the ordinary talk that occurs between Miss Brodie and the girls into a glorification of the commonplace. Thus, the main influence of Sandy (Sister Helena after taking her vows) during her school days was not literary or political or Calvinism. Rather, it was the commonplaces she learned through everyday discourse with Miss Jean Brodie in her prime.

The Influence of Folklore Myth

Males and females make communicative decisions--whether to talk, what to talk about, and how to talk. The choices they make are based on what they believe about the opposite sex. Myths and cultural lore influence the beliefs that humans share about each other and their relationships. For example, I can recall sayings that my mother told my three sisters and me concerning men, how to behave with men, and relationships with men.

Beverly Romberger is an Assistant Professor in the Department of Communications and Theatre Arts, Susquehanna University, Selinsgrove, Pennsylvania 17870.

'You always let the boy win, even if you're better than him!'
(Message: I should defer to men.)

'If he hits you once, even in fun, he'll hit you again.' (Message: I should avoid men who use physical force in any situation.)

'If you're easy, he won't respect you.' (Message: I should not engage in premarital sex.)

'Men only want one thing!' (Message: Men will only be interested in me for sex.)

'The way you make your bed is the way you'll have to sleep in it.' (Message: I have responsibility for my life and I'll live with the consequences of the decisions I make.)

'Aunt Sophie always said, 'It's better to have a snake coming towards you than your husband if he's drunk!'" (Message: I should not marry a man with a drinking problem.)

'You never air your dirty laundry.' (Message: I should keep personal problems private.)

These statements demonstrate the common beliefs about life that my mother passed on to her daughters. They were also beliefs that her mother passed on to her. (I know because I heard these not only from my mother, but from my grandmother.)

The study of folklore and folk myths provide insights into the common beliefs held by males and females in different cultural groups. Dickson and Goulden in *There are Alligators in Our Sewers and Other American Credos* (1983) discuss the common acceptances passed on from generation to generation:

> From the first stirrings of childhood the American acquires
> an ever-thickening encrustation of ideas, beliefs, and dogma
> that makes life all the simpler. Tribal truths pass to him
> from his elders and his contemporaries, to be assimilated
> into common acceptances, an intellectual shorthand that
> enables him to pass through life with a minimum of mental
> effort. (p. xiii)

The "tribal truths" or "common acceptances" include the beliefs males and females hold about each other. Although a wealth of information exists in folklore research about diverse cultural groups, little is known about women and their expressive behavior. (For a current bibliography concerning women and folklore see DeCaro.) In *Spiders and Spinsters* (1982), Weigle focuses on women and mythology. However, not much is known.

> Women **and** mythology, women **in** mythology: we know more about the latter. As generally understood and undertaken, mythology--the study of sacred symbols, texts, rites, and their dynamic expression in human psyches and societies--concerns **men's** myths and rituals. Most extant documents, field data, and interpretations come from male scribes, scholars, artists, and "informants." Thus we know a fair amount about women **in** mythology, about the female figures who people men's narratives, enactments, philosophies and analyses, and almost nothing about women **and** mythology, or women's mythologies--the stories they recount among themselves and in the company of young children, the rituals they perform, and their elaboration, exegesis, and evaluation of their own and men's profoundly moving and significant symbolic expressions. (p. vii)

In her chapter "Appreciating the Mundane: Women and Mythology," Weigle further discusses the need for a revaluation of women's folklore and mythology of the mundane affairs, concerns, and activities that are often practical, immediate, and ordinary:

> This revaluation should contribute to a deeper awareness of the powerful worlds created by gossip and legend, by women considering their own and the lives of those around them, by women telling each other, often privately, about the strange and not-so-strange, the actual, the plausible and the incredible in their physical, interpersonal and intrapersonal lives. (p. 298)

Recent studies are attempting to change the male orientation in folklore scholarship by giving attention to women performers and women's genres. In 1986, a special issue of *Women's Studies International Forum* was edited on women and folklore. The volume focuses on women as 'folk', women in folklore, and women as folklorists (Webster, p. 219). Jordan and Kalcik (1985) present a collection of studies about women's lore, resulting in "... the uneasy (for some) feeling that all is not as it seems, that the student must look beyond ready assumptions and superficial interpretations (p. xi)." Their collection points to aspects of female culture which could be misinterpreted if not examined carefully. One assumption relates directly to this study -- the power of women:

> One assumption that a thoughtful examination of women's culture disproves is that women are necessarily powerless. The chapters in this book [*Women's Folklore, Women's Culture*] do not depict women as victims or as failures in an essentially male world. Despite male domination of one sort or another, many of the women studied here are very much in control of themselves and their worlds, and a sense of real power is communicated by their folklore (p. xii).

Di Leonardo (1987) also observed women's power over their world when studying women and kin work. She found:

> Thus for my women informants, as for most American women, the domestic domain is not only an arena in which unpaid labor must be undertaken but also a realm in which one may attempt to gain human satisfactions - and power - not available in the labor market (p. 451).

Women's expressive behavior concerning their power is the focus of this study. Specifically I examine: **What are the commonplaces females learn about power in relationships with men? Where are they learned and how do women use them?** The speech communication context of this study is based in audience analysis. Speakers analyze their audience and select the sayables based on their beliefs about the audience. Thus, women will make decisions about what to say and how to say it based on their commonplaces about men and power. This study is an attempt to secure data about basic commonplaces and how they affect women's discourse.

Method

Oral histories were collected from eight women of different regions, affiliations, ages, occupations, and family status. Interviewees were tape recorded during the actual interview which lasted from three hours to nine hours. The tape recordings were outlined. Information specifically pertaining to categories concerning power in relationships was transcribed word for word from the recordings. Transcriptions were analyzed to answer (1) what the commonplaces are; (2) who the sources of influence are that communicate the commonplaces; and (3) in what form the commonplaces are communicated.

Interviewees

Participants were recruited through women's community groups, professional organizations, and personal acquaintances. Brief descriptions of the interviewees follow:

SARAH is 66 years old and lives in a small, rural town. Her mother was a garment factory worker and her father a coal miner. Sarah began working at the age of 16 and worked all of her life as a barroom owner and garment factory worker. Sarah divorced her first husband after 11 years and has been married 30 years to her second husband. She has no children.

ANN is 63 years old and lives in an urban area. Her mother was a housewife and her father a machinist. Ann is a Protestant and has worked over 30 years as a secretary. She has been married for 42 years and has no children.

DONNA is 57 years old and lives in a small coalmining town. She was raised Irish Catholic by her mother who was a housewife and her father who was a banker. Donna has worked as a nurse for 30 years and been married for 36 years. She has a son and a daughter.

BETTY is 46 years old. She was raised in the suburbs of a large, metropolitan city by her mother who was a teacher and her father who was a musician. Betty was married to a minister for 18 years before divorcing him. She works in sales and has a son and daughter. She attends a Baptist church.

SUE is 37 years old and lives in a small town. Her mother was a teacher and her father a coal miner. She has worked as a factory and clerical worker. Sue has been married for 18 years and has an adopted son. She is a Protestant.

INEZ is 34 years old. She was raised in an urban area in a strong Roman Catholic, eastern European family. Her mother is a housewife and her father a teacher. Inez has a doctorate degree and is married.

MARIA is 32 years old and lives in a metropolitan area. Maria was raised in an Italian-American family by her mother who was a housewife and her father who was a businessman. Maria has not practiced Catholicism since was 19 years old. Maria has her doctorate and is divorced after six years of marriage. She has no children.

PEG is 27 years old and lives in the rural countryside. Peg was raised on a farm with nine brothers and sisters in a strong German culture. Peg has been married one year and is a Born Again Christian.

Commonplaces Concerning Power in Interpersonal Relationships

Findings of the study indicate that commonplaces exist concerning power in interpersonal relationships. All eight women described power issues in reporting their life histories. The beliefs centered on a man's power, a woman's power, competition from other women, conflict and communication. The individual commonplaces are underlined in the text. The vernacular language is presented without editing.

A man's power. Seven women talked about a man having the power in the relationship. Messages were received by six women about a man's direct control: **the man has to be in control, the man makes the decisions, a man's decision should not be questioned, you do what the man says you do, the woman should follow the man, you let the man win, the man plays to win, there's no way to win with a man, so just keep your mouth shut.** Women described getting these messages from media, husbands, priests, fathers, mothers, and girlfriends. Sue reports in detail learning about the man's power from her husband:

> I learned that you shouldn't question a man. See, I have so many mixed feelings now when I look back. I have bitter feelings, really.... It seemed to be the right thing [when we were dating] to have one boyfriend, to do as he said. There was never anything for me, that I wanted to do. One time, he took me to a prom ... cause I begged him and begged him. And he did take me, but it was awful.... I was just satisfied at the time that I could be with him. Now it seems like so little.
> I learned that you do what the man says you do. You go where he wants to go, what he wants to do. But at the time I was happy with that. I thought that was the thing to do and that's what I did. I got that impression from him because it would always be, "We're going to the drive-in tonight." And I just didn't question it. I think I learned that early in the relationship. Maybe I would suggest about going here or there. Well, he didn't [want to] do that. We were going to do this. I was just glad to be with him so if that's what we were gonna do, then that's what we'd do. And that was fine with me.

I learned from my experiences with Dave [husband]. I argued a few times and there was no way to win. I learned after that ... to shut up. And after a while, I learned not to question. I believed that's how it was.... I really was blind and couldn't see....

I couldn't make any demands of Dave. None. I remember trying different things and he would say no and that was it. I remember wanting to go to different things and he'd say "No, we're not going to do that." I remember being disappointed, but I accepted that was the way it was. I thought if I want to be with him, that's what I'll do. Because at the time, there was competition [another girl] ... and I would just do anything to hang on to him. So, I believed to keep Dave, I had to do what he wanted. And at the time, I just was so madly in love with him that that made it right. I just wanted to be with him. I would sit in his car for hours sometimes waiting for him to come [out of the barroom]. Now I can't believe I did that. ... I never questioned who did the deciding....

After we were married I argued with Dave. I remember saying, "Why can't we?" and him saying, "I don't like doing that." And we used to have many arguments. But I just used to positively give up because there is just no arguing. Because things would get so turned around that I'd be the guilty one. And I didn't even know how it would be turned around, but that's how it would end up. So I could never win. I still never questioned it [husband's power]. I didn't see other people's marriages, except the family's [Dave's relatives]. And I thought that's how it is. [The women in Dave's family told me], "This is how it is. They [the men] make the decisions. They do what they want." And you know, at the time, I just thought we'll [women] ... do whatever they [men] do.

Sue reveals more of the perceptions of the man's power when describing her mother's reaction to how her husband treated her:

[My feelings changed about my husband.] The first few years, he wasn't coming home [after work]. I'd make meals; he wouldn't show up. He just couldn't settle down. And then, the first two years there was so much happening because Mother was sick. Well, Daddy had died. Mother got sick, and I was wrapped up going up there, taking care of her.

And once in a while she'd let things out just by accident, really. Because she would never say anything. But I remember her saying, 'Doesn't he do anything for you.' I remember that so well. And something that has shocked me that I just can't get over, my sister-in-law Kathy told me just last year how Mother cried to her and said, 'I just don't want her to marry him; it's never gonna work.' I never knew that! It just shocked me! I said, 'Kathy, why didn't you ever tell me?' She said, 'What good would it have done.' 'But," she said, 'I'll never forget your Mother crying the night of your wedding rehearsal....' That's the one thing I remember her [Mother] saying; 'Doesn't he do anything for you....'

One time she [Mother] asked if we'd take her to a drum and bugle competition.... And I begged Dave and that time he consented. So we went. And I don't know, whenever we did anything at home, if we went to something like that, you'd normally stop to eat a meal then either before or after. You don't just go and come home. And I remember Mother saying, 'Now I'll treat. We'll stop at this restaurant.' 'No,' Dave said, 'We'll go home. Sue will make something.' And I remember it was so tense. Cause I knew I wanted to and Mother wanted to. I thought, why can't we. But Dave didn't like to do that. And I didn't question him cause I knew Dave, 'No, we won't do that.' And I didn't wanna argue in front of her. Then we come right home and Dave pulls in at the apartment and said, 'Now, Sue, you can go up and make something.' And Mom said, 'No, you take me home. I'm not hungry.' And I often think of the hurt, and I remember her saying, and it was the second time she said it, 'Doesn't he do anything for you.'

Later on when Sue describes what she would like in a man, she says, "If he treated me well. Not looks. I wouldn't care anymore about looks, if he treated me well."

Betty agrees that the husband makes the decisions. She said, "In our marriage, my husband made the decisions. Always. I thought that was the way it should be." She also describes knowing at a young age to let the man win:

For some reason when you're a little child and you're playing games, the little boy is supposed to win and the little girl is supposed to lose. But I can't remember that anybody told me that. But somewhere I realized that I was supposed to let the little boy win at Monopoly, you know, or Old Maids, and I was supposed to lose.

Maria also agrees that men want to be in control:

> I agree that men have to be in control. That's a real battle with most men. They control you by shutting themselves down emotionally. They won't share. They many times want to make the decisions, be the decision-maker. Ed [ex-husband] told me when we first got married that in his family when his parents couldn't come to a negotiated compromise his father made the decision. And that was the way it was gonna be with us. And I said, "Ha! Bullshit!" And it never was that way. But I think men do wanna be in control a lot because I think they feel it's expected of them. And I think also they don't like relinquishing control.... Men do wanna be in control. And in personal relationships, yea, very much so. And they control you in a lot of ways, especially by becoming silent. That's how they control you the most. I learned that from personal experience.

Women heard the messages, but most disagreed. Maria states,

> My father ... pointed that out [that I should let the man win]. I beat Bobby [boyfriend] at bowling a couple of times and he was always pissed. So my father pointed that out. Popular books, TV shows conveyed it most to me. That if a little girl was too good at things, she was gonna lose the man. And that she had to change.... But I never bought it! I would always compete. I was reinforced for doing well.... There was never a time that I intentionally lost at anything. Well, maybe there was. I'm trying to think back. There might have been some times when I passed up a good opportunity to beat somebody, because I'd beaten them so many times in a game....
> But in fighting, no, you never let the man win. That wasn't modeled for me. My mother always got the upper, the last word, hand. So fighting, no way. You don't let the man win at all.

Peg talks about her views:

> I don't let the man win. A lot of times if I'm right, I'll stick
> to my guns and I won't let him win. I don't even think the
> preacher thinks that. Because I think if the man is wrong he
> ought to admit it. If he gets away with that too much it could
> really change his personality and character. If he gets away
> with murder like that.

Donna says,

> No, you don't let the man win. Never. You give a good fight.
> Fair, but good! It's something I learned ... that a woman has
> every right to win that a man does. We may have to work
> harder at it, but that's OK.

Women got the message that a man wants to be in control, to have the power in
the relationship, to win. But most of the women expressed an unwillingness to
concede the power that they believe men want.

With a similar theme, the women discuss that **a man should be strong,
but not dominating** and **a man should treat the woman as an equal and
respect her thoughts and ideas.** However, qualifying these beliefs is the
commonplace that **a man should not let his wife tell him what to do,** also
expressed by three of the eight women. Ann sums it up best when she says,

> I wouldn't like a husband who would try to dominate me or
> say, 'I'm the boss. You do everything that I say.' I have a
> little bit more of a mind of my own than that. I would want
> it to be a 50-50 proposition. I would want us to decide things
> together, if there were decisions to be made. I wouldn't
> want a husband who, in fact, I don't think I could be married
> to a man who would do that.... I was always a little bit
> independent. Although I wouldn't like a husband whose
> wife could tell him everything to do either. I mean I
> wouldn't like that either. I don't think that's fair.... Because
> that kind of man wouldn't be strong, absolutely not.

Thus, in relationships with men, women want a man to be strong, yet respect
and treat her as an equal. The man who lets his wife dominate is not seen as
desirable.

Two women reported the commonplace that **you can't trust men**. Women
also talked about this in reference to the sex act, which is discussed in the section
on sexual relations. However, Betty and Peg got this message concerning
interpersonal relationships. Betty states,

> My mother portrayed an attitude of, quote, you can't trust
> men, because her father back umpteen years ago had walked
> out on her mother and left them. She'd mention, "Oh, well,
> my father walked out on us."

Peg describes her view of men:

> But there's something about men. I really don't trust men.
> It's not nice to say. You're supposed ... to trust. But there's
> something within me, if I'm to be honest, that I really don't
> trust 'em.

The sources women mentioned about a man's power were numerous.
Women said they heard messages from television, movies, books, fathers, mothers, other women, girlfriends, priests, relatives, and personal experience. The
forms reported were directives, observation, and gossip.

A woman's power. Five women talked about a woman's power. Three
women believed that **the woman usually gets her way**. Betty remembers
when her parents disagreed, her mother won, eventually. Inez says of her
mother, "My Mom believes you let Dad think he's won, but he really hasn't. So
there's some deviousness about that." **Maria** describes the women in her home-
town:

> My father didn't have a lot of control. My mother had all the
> control. The women I was raised with had a tremendous
> amount of control in their marriages. And they have a
> tremendous amount of decision-making authority, as you'll
> find in Italian-American families. The woman is tremen-
> dously powerful. She may assume a traditional role of
> housekeeper, but as far as decision-making and money-han-
> dling she's got a lot of power. Definitely.

Three women believe that **a woman has a right to her own views**. Donna
exemplified this when talking about her relationship with her future husband:

> We did a lot of fighting. I think it was maybe that I was not
> the kind of person that Ken [future husband] was used to.
> His mother was the typical submissive wife, and his father
> was the boss. And I was not about to be bossed.... I knew I
> had the right to say what I felt and have someone listen to
> me. They didn't have to agree with me, but at least listen
> to me.
> I think it was our independence in our family.... My mother
> influenced my life a great deal.... Mother taught us all that

we were individuals and had rights.... As long as I can
remember I was taught to be independent and to respect
people in authority, my elders. But not to revere them,
respect them. They're not always right.

Three women also stated that **women compete with men**. The women
recounted that as children they competed in sports. Donna describes this:

> [In school boys and girls were segregated] but at home in the
> neighborhood I lived in boys and girls played together. We
> played baseball, football, all kinds of games. Some in each
> others' homes. Even Monopoly was known way back in the
> years when I was growing up. We played cards. There was
> no such thing as the boys played with the boys. And there
> were about 20 of us in the neighborhood. And we all played
> together. The boys got mad if they didn't win, but so did the
> girls. If the girls lost, we went home in a huff; if the boys
> lost, they went home in a huff. And sometimes it would get
> very physical. You'd get bumped in the back from someone
> you walked by. But it was good, clean fun.
> I was never told, "Don't do this because it isn't ladylike." As
> long as we were dressed appropriately for the sport, there
> didn't seem to be any problem. Some of my girlfriends were
> not [allowed to do things]. There were several games that
> would involve running on the back street and what have you
> and they were not allowed. You know, "If someone sees you
> coming out the alley, what will they think." And we talked
> about that at home--that you can do in the front street
> anything you can do in the back street, if you wanna do it.

Maria describes competing in sports,

> Fifth grade summer was a real important time for me.
> That's when I started to become part of the neighborhood
> gang. And it just seemed like there were thousands of kids
> that played together because there were all these families
> that had two up to seven, eight kids. So there were all these
> families in my neighborhood, tons of kids and we all gathered
> in this yard and played kickball every night. During the day
> I either went to the pool swimming or I hung around with
> my girlfriends. But at night, we were out there with the
> boys. And we were on kickball teams. And I was on Ken's
> team. Ken was my implicit boyfriend.... And we used to play

the blue and the gold team. And we had these intensely competitive kickball games. The guys were just real serious about winning.... I was forced to learn to compete.

Inez describes competing in intellectual ways,

> I remember feeling competitive with men as a child in parochial school, especially in math.... [Today] I always try to beat a man at sports. Well, I never could at sports. But if it's anything like Trivial Pursuit I can be very competitive. I think it's more in intellectual ways. I would never let a personal relationship wanna make me feel, try to down peddle [my ability to win].

Two women expressed that **a woman expects to be treated** as an equal. Donna clarifies this best:

> I don't fear anything from a man. I expect them to treat me as an equal.... And if what I'm telling them [the doctors] is gonna help them in the practice and help them get their patients out, then all I ask is that they accept that fact [I'm an equal]....
> I think that we as women have got to do something to change our image. I don't know if ERA is the answer. I don't believe in burning bras; I don't know that women should always be expected to perform the same things as men and serve in the army. I don't know if I believe in all of those things. But I think it's time that women are [equal]. Take a look at most of the households. There's two working people in most households, the man and the wife. And we'll never be equal in salary.... But women ... want to be treated not as the subservient or the scullery maid.... I still like a man to open the door for me.... I like someone to help me on with my coat. But I don't expect 'cause he does that that he's gonna expect me to lay down and be his rug.

Women believe a woman has power. They believe women often get their way, have a right to their own views, can compete with men, and should be treated as equals. Few sources of forms were reported. Personal experience and observing mothers and other women were mentioned.

Competition from other women. Four women talked about competition from other women. Three women believe **other women are a threat to**

keeping your man. Peg refers to this at different times throughout her interview. She believes men can be tempted and that women can lose their man:

> I saw her as a big threat 'cause she [a girl in high school] was busty.... She wasn't feminine except for she was built. And Sam [future husband] saw that quality in her.... I thought I'm gonna lose him. I'm gonna lose him just like the rest [former boyfriends]. This is what was going through my mind.... And I always thought of women as threats as long as they were built. That's how I thought....
> What I fear is losing him. Losing him to someone sexier or younger or even someone who's listening more than me. Sometimes I feel guilty 'cause I think well, maybe I am too busy doing everything else that I'm not listening....
> She [my sister] said she wanted a guy that was gonna stick home, like a self-employed guy, which I looked for.... 'Cause I always thought that when they [men who work away from home] have to travel to go to work and they see these women, who knows what they're doing. If they stop at barrooms on the way, who knows. I never wanted a guy that drank 'cause I said that keeps them out of the temptation [of women] in the barroom.

Peg believes that a **woman should not break up another woman's marriage.** She states,

> I know my girlfriend [in junior high] was supposed to have been involved with one of the teachers, the science teacher, in a sexual way. After school and stuff like that. Meeting him at places. And he was a married man.... But my girlfriend told me right out that she was having an affair with him.... I don't like breaking up marriages. I don't believe in it. I don't believe that anybody should break up someone else's marriage. If the marriage is already broken up, it may be a totally different story. But like [this woman I know who's living with a married man] ... other women don't think too much of her. But I don't think it's her personality as much as what she's done. 'Cause she split the family up.

Two women discuss territoriality regarding men. Maria stated that in high school girls believed **a girlfriend should not steal another girlfriends's guy:**

Another thing that was really important to girls was that we
didn't steal each other's men. And I think I stole one [boy-
friend] of Mary's [a girlfriend] one time and boy, she hated
me for days. She really did. Or I started to go out with
someone she liked. But for the most part, Barbara [a close
friend] and I just respected each other's territory. There
wasn't much intrusion on each other's territory.
[What made a boy your territory was that] . . . you already
went out or verbalized to other women that you liked this
guy and you wanted him to be yours. And it was a real taboo
to infringe on other people's territory. [Even if the guy
hadn't expressed interest in you] that was still not the thing
to do. It was kind of like undercutting. This really went on
mostly through Barbara and me in sophomore and junior
year. Barbara was a real big influence on me in how I related
to men. And we just had our standards. In fact, she didn't
like the fact that before Bob and I, her brother, even got
together that Ruth [a former friend] . . . was after Bob. And
Barbara felt Ruth was after Bob just to compete with me and
not because she really liked Bob. Throughout high school
there was a certain respect. And there were so many stable
couples during high school . . . and you had a boyfriend and
stuck with that boyfriend for at least a year or two. And you
just didn't intrude. There was really no boyfriend stealing
going on. If a girl came on to a boyfriend of another girl, that
was something that lowered her status in the group. It really
did . . . Guys would use that [a girl coming on] to make their
girlfriends jealous and it worked. So they [guys] communicated that but in a manipulative way. There was a purpose
to it, and it worked.

Peg believes **you can't trust girlfriends where men are concerned** and
describes what happened to her:

He [boyfriend] did something that was really smart assed.
Oh, my best girlfriend. Do you believe it! Kate. We weren't
totally broken up yet. And he said to Brad [Kate's boy-
friend], "Hey, I'll trade Peg for Kate anytime." And this got
back to me and I thought, my best friend Kate! And I started
hating her. It made me mad at her. I thought he wants her.
Then, I thought , no this isn't the way to feel. I shouldn't be
mad at her 'cause she's my best friend. He wants her. Then
I found out later she went out with him! This is my best

girlfriend! She said, "Oh, he's really neat." She and Brad weren't getting along so she went out with Rick [my boyfriend]. After all the things I confided in her! See, I used to tell her things before I told Mom. So I got to the point where I thought I'm not trusting any of my girlfriends anymore. I'm gonna tell my Mom. I did. Because Nancy [another friend] did the same thing with Howard and I used to tell Carol. And those are the two that went after him [Howard] after we broke up.

It's a funny thing. 'Cause you tell them everything and it seems they know him [the man] better than you do. They know him just as good. And they know all his weaknesses; they know all his strengths. And they go back and can be the person he wants them to be because they know what things he didn't like about me. So she didn't drink in front of him and he really respected that. Everything! Figure it out, though. If you tell someone about a person enough, like really open up, that person seems to know them. They know what that person wants ... and can play up to be what that person wants. And it pissed me off 'cause that's exactly what she [girlfriend] done. I didn't trust Kate or Nancy or Carol.... You don't know who to trust when you're young.... They were my girlfriends and acted like that. But Mom always told me, she said, "You know, maybe they weren't your girlfriends." She said, "You hung around with the wrong kind of crowd." Which I did. I hung around with wild girls.

Four women talked about competition from other women. They believe other women threaten keeping their man, that women should not break up marriages, and that girlfriends shouldn't, but often do, steal boyfriends. Few sources or forms were reported. Personal experience was most frequently stated.

Conflict and Communication. A final area of beliefs relating to the politics of interpersonal relationships is conflict. Four women talked about disagreements. Peg recalls her parents fighting over her:

Mom and Dad would fight. I'd hear Mom say, "You're always picking on Peg! Why don't you just let her alone for once!" Mom would always stick up for me.... Mom supported me. Mom never really told me what to do, she just supported me through everything I did. Like every time I made a mistake, she picked me up when I was ready to fall apart.

Inez recalls how her parents fought:

My parents never fought in terms of yelling at one another. Basically, Dad would get angry, make some sort of statement. And Mom would say something that was nonsatisfactory. And then Dad would go off in a sulk. That's how they would fight. It was never resolved. It was just not dealt with.

Sue doesn't remember her parents fighting.

I never saw them fight. I don't think I ever did. I remember them disagreeing. And it always would be about if he didn't come right in the house. Like we lived in hotel city. He wasn't a drinker, but he would like to go in to play pool in the firehouse right in back of our house. And he'd go in there to talk with the men. I don't even know if he ever drank a beer. But maybe. Mostly just socialize. And those are the only arguments I remember them having. She'd be mad at him that he'd get lost and you know, wouldn't be home in the evening to spend time there. That's the only thing I remember. I'm not saying they never argued, but if they did, they never argued in front of us.

Ann states,

My parents had a good marriage. I don't remember fights. I remember disagreements. He was never violent. I can remember them disagreeing on things. If they did fight, it was when we weren't around, you know. As far as making a scene, never....
My mother usually won. I think so. Eventually, it might not be right at that moment, but eventually. And she was usually right. My father was rather stubborn. So he thought he was always right and I don't think he was always right.
They usually fought over things we [children] were supposed to do or not supposed to do. The kids more than anything. If we were told to do something and didn't do it....
Never over money.... Things around the home and the house and we kids.

One woman reported a saying she was told about regarding conflict in a marriage, **don't let the sun go down on your wrath**. Sue explains:

> The only advice I remember [being told before marriage] ...
> was from Mammy Snyder [Dave's mother] at my [bridal]
> shower. And one of the things was you had to write down a
> saying, something that would help the bride. And Mammy
> wrote ... "Don't let the sun go down on your wrath." Or
> something like that. I don't remember the exact words, but
> it was don't go to bed mad. And I used to try to remember
> that. It stuck in my head. 'Cause I used to think, I don't
> want him [Dave] to wake up dead and that I went to bed
> mad. I used to try to remember that.

Women reported conflict and also communication skills they want in a man. Six women spoke about communication skills they want. Three women said **a man should be verbally intimate, able to share his feelings and experiences**, and three women believe **a man should be genuinely interested in conversation with the woman.** Ann explains,

> I looked for ... someone who could hold a conversation with
> me.... Bill [husband] isn't a big talker. In fact, he often
> laughs. When we were first married, Bill and I can commu-
> nicate but he doesn't do an awful lot of talking. And he still
> tells me about when we were first married I used to say,
> 'Hold conversation with me! Talk to me!' We'd just sit there
> sometimes. But I don't want to mislead you, because it isn't
> that we don't communicate and we do have a good relation-
> ship. But he is not a big talker. He doesn't just sit down and
> talk for the sake of talking. If he has something to say, he
> says it. But other than that we don't have a lot of conversa-
> tion, as such. We do more since we're older than we did
> when we were first married. But he said I just said, 'Hold
> conversation with me!'

> 'Cause we talked and communicated pretty well at home
> always. There was always someone around. My mother and
> dad, brothers, sisters.... I just couldn't get used to the fact
> that he [Bill] would just sit there and not talk.

> His father was not a talker at all, and his mother was
> somewhat, but not to a great extent.... In fact his father
> would leave and go to work and not even say 'good-bye,' or
> 'I'm going.' He just didn't like to say good-bye; he would not
> say good-bye. And he'd just disappear. And when I would
> be at Bill's house I'd say, 'Well where's your father?' And

Bill would say, 'Well he went to work.' And I'd say, 'Well he didn't say anything.' He never did.... Bill knew that I was so amazed at his father, so he [Bill] always said good-bye and kissed me when he went to work. But I thought that [his Dad's behavior] was the strangest thing. My Dad always kissed my mother good-bye before he left the house. So I was used to that. Bill wasn't, but he did it.

Inez also wanted a husband who likes to talk and explains the deficit in her own marriage:

And I wanted someone who was genuinely interested in conversation. And I don't really see Ted all that interested in sitting down and talking. I think we fall into the habit of turning the television on, and the two of us look at the tube, rather than look at each other and talk. And if there's nothing on TV, that's a terrible night. Heaven forbid it would just be us two. It's scary, almost.

Two women said that **a man should listen and be supportive, comforting to the woman**. Maria describes her conversations with her girlfriend Ruth:

Ruth, who was my very close friend in college, and I talked about it, about what we wanted from our husband. That we wanted them to listen to us and comfort us. But somehow I looked at Ed [future husband] and said, 'Well, he doesn't do that so much now.' Ed's reassurance was like, this is the way Ed reassured me anytime I was in a crisis, 'Don't sweat the small stuff,' or he would cut me off with, 'Ah, what are you making a big deal out of that for?' So I viewed Ed as someone who would grow with marriage and become a better person, a better husband. Ruth married a guy who looked like Robert Redford, but was an asshole. And was abusive.... So we talked about what we wanted in marriage, but the ideas were very fuzzy, abstract....

Later, Maria comments on what she's looking for in a man and again refers to communication skills:

I want to be able to rely on a man for some support and comfort. I want him to be able to provide emotional support. I want his friendship.... I want a lot of interaction. I want a lot of talking. A lot of spontaneity between the two of us.

Two women said they believe that some women and men think males shouldn't cry or show emotions. The women disagreed and explained that **a man should show his emotions**. Donna talks about men having to be in control of their emotions:

> I've heard my friends say that men don't show how they feel. Men cry, and it's good for men to cry. I think it's very important that a man shows the same emotions as a woman in the same situation. I think it's real important. If they don't, then they can't really have feelings for the person. I keep thinking of when my mother died.... Ken [husband] and I had a very bad morning before she died. And we sat in the lounge and we both cried, and at that time my parish priest came. And he sat between us and talked to us about what death was and that we should consider it as a highway and it has its holes and its potholes and its curves ... and 'til it was all done we were all crying. The priest, my husband, myself. And it was so good for all of us. It really was. Sometimes tears do clear the brain. I have seen my son cry. I've seen him cry when he's happy. And I think that's just as important as crying when you're unhappy.

Two women talked about wanting **a husband who would spend time talking with the children and agree on parenting responsibilities**. Sue wants her husband to want the same things for their child:

> I wish he would want the same things for Kevin [son]. I have high goals. Dave [husband] goes to 'Well, it was good enough for me. He has more than I do. That should be good enough.' It isn't good enough. I want more. Like Kevin wants to be a lawyer. He got a letter from the Andersonville Bar Association to join this club. Dave said, 'You don't wanna do that, have to drive to Andersonville [30 minute drive].' I said, 'Yes, I do.' I want him [son] to go. He'll know then if this is what he wants. He [Dave] left me go, but I can tell it's killing him because I have to drive him [son] to Andersonville. But if we stay in the valley, there's nothing.... I could see Kevin [son] even getting into a rut. And I don't wanna push him the wrong way, but he needs a push. At first he wasn't sure he wanted to go, 'Well, if no one else [at school] is going.' I said, 'Kevin, you just can't wait for everyone else. If they all jump in a river, you can't do it, you know.' And then another

> guy did go along, and they have their second meeting tomor-
> row night and he said, 'You know I really want to be an
> officer, that would be great.' And I'm so glad.... But Dave
> thinks he got an apple for Christmas, Kevin gets three
> things, that's too much. But times are changed. There
> again, we're from two different backgrounds. I got lots for
> Christmas, sometimes too much. And I think you can give
> too much, but I think you can keep it a minimum. But I want
> more for Kevin, and Dave and I don't agree. I think we
> should have similar goals for children.

Women want a man to have communication skills. They want the man to be
verbally intimate, to be genuinely interested in talking to women, to express
their emotions, to be a supportive listener, and to talk to their children and share
similar goals for their children.

The few instances where sources for the beliefs were expressed concerning
communication skills included girlfriends and personal experience. When forms
were mentioned, gossip was used to convey the commonplaces.

All eight women talked about power in relationships. The commonplaces
focused on a man's power, a woman's power, competition from other women,
and conflict and desired communication skills. Sources mentioned were media,
husbands, priests, fathers, mothers, girlfriends, other women, and personal
experience. Observation, gossip, directives, and sayings were the forms.

Commonplaces Concerning Power in Sexual Relations

Eight women reported commonplaces about power concerning the sex act.
Beliefs focused on a woman's power, men's sexual needs, and competition from
other women.

A woman's power. All eight women heard the saying **it's up to the
girl to say no.** Donna stated,

> I've heard it's up to the girl and I do believe it. I told both
> my son and daughter to think of themselves, their self-re-
> spect. What was it going to do? What changes would it make
> in their life? I really feel a lot of girls, a lot of women use as
> an excuse what could they do because they're only a woman,
> you know. And I can't buy that.

Sarah said,

> Well, I think so [it's up to the girl]. I feel that's the way it
> is. Like heavy petting, in the first place. Or leading a guy

on, making him think you'll have sex with him when you don't want to.

Maria reported,

> 'Yea, it's up to the girl. That old thing that men fostered that they couldn't help themselves. And women had more will power and they really bore the whole responsibility of intercourse. That if they let that happen it was their responsibility. The fall of Eve kind of thing. Yes, I have heard that. I've heard it implicitly and I've heard it explicitly. "You make your bed, you've got to lie in it."

Inez said,

> I've definitely heard that it isn't something that you can blame men for. That the girl gets herself in trouble.... I expected that it would be me who had to stop. I really expected a man to go as far as he could. I think I expected all men to!

Two women reported hearing **you don't have to do anything: you can say no**. Peg said,

> Mom said, "You can say no!" Then my sisters said, "Yea, but not if they drop you off along a road!" They always said, "Always wait till you're closer to home. If they wanna put their arm around you or something, try to get close to home 'cause you never know. If they go on a back, wiggly road, stay on your own side." I was warned, now that I think of it. I was warned to stay on my own side [of the car]. And always watch where you're going, too, because you never know. They could say you're real far away from home. And maybe you're only a hop, skip, and a jump away, and you didn't know....
> Mom told me, "You don't have to do anything." I know the last guy I dated, Karl, said that. He respects a girl. He said, "It's always up to the girl." He would never force a girl to make love.

Maria got these messages:

All the nuns considered themselves the brides of Christ. In the Franciscan order they got married to Christ. They wore wedding gowns. At a certain point when they were full-fledged nuns. And the priests told us that we were to follow the man. In fact, even when I got married, the priest told us in our conference [before the marriage ceremony]. So the priests were telling us that. The nuns really weren't.
The nuns never really said that! And Sister Anna told us, "No way! If a guy wants you to do something and you don't wanna do it, then you have every right to say no." Oh, yea. Sister Anna was different. And that's what got her in trouble. Sister Anna was only around for a year. She battled the others; she didn't fit in at all. The others would just kind of shut up and did their jobs. And Anna was a real ball of fire. She was a really little lady, like four, nine. I liked her. Sister Anna told us that if men wanted us to do sexual things on dates, we didn't have to if we didn't want to. We just didn't have to do it. And petting led to intercourse. That was the thing she told us girls. And we talked about that a lot. We really did, in religion class. That if you started to French kiss it immediately led to intercourse, which showed her naivete.

A final commonplace about a woman's power was stated by Maria. She read in a magazine article that **a woman had more power in the relationship if she can withhold sex for a while.** Maria was the only woman who stated this belief.

The sources reported were girlfriends, nuns, mother, media, and men. The forms were sayings, gossip, and directives.

Men's Sexual Needs. All eight women heard statements about a man's sex drive. Numerous commonplaces were reported about men's needs. Eight women heard that **men are all alike; they want only one thing.** Eight women reported that **a man will go as far as he can with a woman.** Six women said they heard **what man wouldn't take it if it was pushed in his face.** Three women believe **a man can't help himself; he has to have his sexual needs satisfied.** And one woman learned **you can't trust men.**

Sarah revealed:

[My Dad had affairs with women] and then I guess from there you just get the idea that that's [sex] what a man wants with a woman. A man's after sex. When I was about 14 years old I had a girlfriend who used to sleep with me a lot. And my older brother used to come over in our bedroom and coax her to get into bed with him. But he was three years older, you know. He was like 17, and we were 14, or we were 15. And he was 18, you know. I knew what he was after. And my girlfriend surely did know, too. She used to tell him to clear out. And then I got the idea that that's all a man wants is sex....

Inez reported:

There's a part of me that thinks men want, often, they just want sex and don't want any other part of the relationship. And that's based on when I returned to graduate school. I didn't date for a while. And then I dated three men in my first year. And all of them tried to get me to go to bed. And I just couldn't believe it. I told them no. And no one called me back. They left in a huff. Each one of them. And I thought men just want one thing. That's what I thought they did. And I decided these were graduate students ... And were just horny as hell.... None of them were interested in me. I mean we had a great time on our dates. But they all wanted to go to bed, and I said no and that was that. So that was really disheartening.

Donna said:

I heard that [what man wouldn't take it if it was pushed in his face] from my peers. It was getting at that if a girl was going to come on to a man and make it quite evident to him that she was all his, I mean he was not going to turn his back. I think that's true. I believe that the average man, if he would be honest, would say yes [he would have sex with a woman if she was willing].

Maria stated:

I've heard that men only want one thing. From friends when they were disgruntled with their relationships or trying to cope with some kind of rejection, 'that men only wanted sex with me.' I've heard it from older women who I feel didn't really have mature relationships with their men. Like Lois, my mother's friend, 'Men only want one thing. That's it....'

I heard that [what man wouldn't take it if it was pushed in his face] dozens of times. A man not being responsible for fidelity because a woman threw herself at him. I didn't hear that from my mother. She had some real high standards about fidelity. She didn't tolerate running around at all. She'd kill my father. She'd say, "I'll kill him! I'll cut his nuts off!" She viewed the man very much as responsible for fidelity, my mother did.

I've heard that from friends who maybe didn't have a good sense of themselves as women. And, 'Well of course he had to because she threw herself at him. How could he resist.' Women talking about their boyfriends infidelity, I've heard that.

Peg said:

Yea, I've heard that many a time [that men only want one thing]. Friends used to say it. I used to always hear my friends say they're only after one thing. The preacher used to say, 'Don't, don't, don't, don't.' That was the one that when we [husband and I] went through counseling he kept saying don't do this and don't do that. And I heard that on the radio a lot too, that men want your body. I've read it in books. Just about everywhere. And my sisters used to say [about guys]. 'They only wanted one thing!....'

Mom always warned me what men are like.... It seemed like she took it out on Daddy, men are alike! She must have put a lot of that into my head. Although I learned it myself. I believe it. Maybe your man isn't like that, but I think men cheat on their wives. It makes you wonder....

When asked if she ever heard the saying, "What man wouldn't take it if it was pushed in his face," Peg replied:

They'd all take it if it was pushed in his face! Dad would say that, every man. My brothers would say, 'Hey, if they're gonna show it, might as well.' My older brother would say any man would. He would tell me that. Bruce [younger brother] would say that. My Dad would say that. I don't know if my uncles would say that, the ones that are living with us. Men. Men usually say it, 'What man wouldn't take it!' I'd say that to Sam [husband]. And Tom [brother-in-law] had a big influence on me there. He used to tell us [women in the family] all the time that we worried about the dumbest things. Then Gail [my sister and his wife] would go, 'Well, would you?' And then we'd bring up [hypothetically] this beautiful girl that would be coming out of the shower. Because he goes to people's places in the morning early or if people call him late at night. [He's an electrician.] You know, and if they're ready for bed. And he'd come home and say different things about the way these women are dressed, and some have a robe on. And they'd compliment him.... And Gail would question him. She's not jealous though. But she'd question him. And I'd think oh my gosh, I'd kill him for that! But he'd be honest with her and see, Sam [my husband] won't be honest with me because I am jealous.

Peg describes in detail learning that **you can't trust men**. She learned this from her sisters:

My oldest sister had an awful lot of influence on me with men. Because she is divorced. And she had gone with a guy. She was in love with a guy. She was strictly, totally in love with this guy. His name was Barry. And they broke up. And I knew this from hearsay and she'd be telling Mom if only she would have given in she would have kept him. But because she didn't, he couldn't take it anymore. And I got a lot of my ideas and views from her.

And Shirley [another sister] had a lot of bad experiences with guys. One time her and Sally [another sister] were together. And I heard this 'cause I'm the little kid listening, but, I didn't understand men yet. And I remember her saying, 'You can't trust men!' She said, 'If you go away, don't say no to em till you get em home.' In other words lead him on until you get him closer to home. Because one time they were in a mountain somewhere and he said, "Either you're gonna give in or get out.' And they were so scared they didn't wanna get out cause they knew they couldn't walk home, it was late at night. And they were really frightened, but they wouldn't do it to give in. And they got out. And I guess the guys came back for em later on, never to date them again, but they were doing this as a scare tactic.

Two commonplaces were stated abut a man's power in the sexual act--a man **feels more manly if he can satisfy the woman sexually** and the male ego **is fragile when it comes to sex.** Peg conveyed these beliefs while narrating her advice to a woman:

> Men should be able to satisfy women.... I said open up to him. You don't have to talk at first. Let him know. Don't make it look like it's something he's not doing. 'Cause men are funny! Right away they think, "Oh, I'm not giving it to you enough! I'm not good enough!" You've got to be so careful with 'em. You've got to know what he's thinking, too. You've got to be sensitive to him. Because males, "That's where I'm good. In bed! That's one thing I can do for my wife!" I think men want to be good lovers; they want to satisfy. I know of people that have terrible marriages. Yet they say their husband wants to satisfy them in bed. In an utterly ridiculous situation, you wouldn't even think they go to bed! I can name the people. I said, "He ridicules you. He condemns you. He says how ugly you are in front of other people. He says how fat you are and yet when you go to bed he really wants to satisfy you!"

Competition from other women. Peg stated three commonplaces about female competition. The statements were mentioned by Peg only. But she received the messages from several sources. Peg believed that **other women are a threat to keeping your man faithful.** Her report about what repair-men encounter in private homes exemplifies this:

> Women come on to men. They do! Tom's [brother-in-law] already confided and said that when he goes to an electrician's call.... He's come home and said, "Boy, the woman today came right to the door in her bathrobe. And she was real seductive." And I've heard guys that actually told me that they've already had nude, absolutely nude, women open the door. And then the women said something about looking at 'em. "It's OK to look, but don't stare," the women said to 'em. And this was repeated. My brother could tell you stories galore about what the men say at work. And these are men that are going to fix the phone, fix the carpet, anything. But women! Women are like that today. My husband's gonna definitely be self-employed! 'Cause I know it's happening!

Peg recounted an episode with her boyfriend Howard:

> I found this out after the party was over. He wouldn't let
> me drink [at the party]. He didn't want me to do this 'cause
> I was special. He didn't want a wife that was gonna be like
> that. See he always led me to believe that we were gonna
> get married. 'Cause he'd say he don't want a wife that's
> gonna be drinking.
> And that same night when I walked out the room and was
> entertaining other people ... he was making flirtations with
> this other girl. And I heard after the party that he was up
> her pants. But she was really flirting with him, too. And
> they said, and I saw it, too, that she had her legs spread for
> him.

Peg stated that **a woman knows if another woman is coming on to her
man:**

> The preacher said jealousy is a sin. But God will let a woman
> know if another woman is coming on to her husband. It's in
> our minds that we should know that. And he said that's not
> jealousy. Sam [husband] said right away when we were
> finding each others' faults [in counseling] and we had to say
> one thing that really bothered us and Sam said right away
> about me being jealous. And I thought oh, my goodness, he
> told the preacher that! That is my biggest fault. And he
> [preacher] said ... "Well, I do wanna tell you that if she can
> sense another woman coming on to you that that's not
> jealousy." Then we got on to something else and never got
> back to it.

Peg reported that **women compete and compare with other women
about their looks, shapes, and sexuality:**

> Probably when I was a teenager if I looked the way I do now
> I wouldn't have had half the dates I had.... My legs, I've got
> cellulose. I'm so self-conscious of my legs.... I'm so ashamed
> of my body.... I can't wear shorts around anybody ... and I
> wonder if other women, sexy women, are thinking, "Boy,
> why is she wearing those shorts with her legs. Look how fat
> they are. They're really ugly." That's what's going through
> my head ...

I think women look at other women and compare themselves. We all do! Most women I talk to say, "Well, I don't
look like this one or I don't look like that one." And I know
a friend and I were just talking recently, and she said, "She's
really built! But she has white legs; we have dark legs." You
know, different things. Yea, you sort of tend to take the
other person and put yourself aside of them. We shouldn't,
but we do.... We sometimes look for their weakness to make
ourselves feel better....

I don't ever do this around men. Like with Sam, if he finds
another girl attractive, I compare myself to her, too. In-
wardly. But I'm not saying to him, "Well, I'm bigger than
she is. Or I'm this." I don't do that around him. I want to
hear what he has to say about her. But I'll go tell my best
friend what he said. And then she'll say, "Yea! I bet my
husband feels the same way, too." And then sometimes we'll
[husband and wife] get in arguments about it.

Eight women reported commonplaces about the power of the sex act. Beliefs
focused on a woman's power, men's sexual needs, and female competition. The
sources reported included girlfriends, other women, mothers, preacher, nuns,
media, men, and personal experiences. The forms were sayings, directives, and
gossip.

Conclusions

The findings reveal several implications. The first is that a bona fide oral
culture exists within women's lives. The oral culture includes private lore that
is passed on from generation to generation of women about relationships and
power. Women's expressive behavior included gossip, sayings, stories, and directives that told them how to behave and what to expect from men. Although the
beliefs were sometimes polarized (e.g., **the man has to be in control** and **the
woman usually gets her way**), women's oral culture conveys messages about
men and women and power. The common denominator when it comes to the
male sex is this: women talk about men a lot.

A second implication is that women learn that sex can be used for economical
and political power. Women believed that men possess insatiable sexual desires.
They have the power to satisfy men's sexual needs or withhold sex. The power,
responsibility, and consequences are with the woman--"It's up to the girl to say
no," "You don't have to do anything," "You made your bed, you've got to lie in it."
Since other women can also satisfy men's sexual needs, they are seen as competition, as a threat to "keeping one's man." Thus, even girlfriends cannot and must
not be trusted where men are concerned.

A third implication is that consensual validation appears to be an important part of women's discourse. Women talked about their talk. Typically women had one or two closest girlfriends. The names of the friends might change, but the structure didn't. The women described in detail checking their reality about power and males. They listened to mothers, nuns, and other women. They checked rules, what a boy would or wouldn't be allowed to do with them. They checked feelings, "This is how I want to be treated. Do you? They checked events, "This happened to me. Did it happen to you?" The commonplaces they believed about men were validated through discourse with significant females.

Psychiatrist Harry Stack Sullivan (1953, p. 249) described adolescent development as a time when a "chum" or close friend of the same sex is sought. Interest in another person quite like oneself appears for validation of personal worth. However, he emphasized that he is speaking rather exclusively of males. My research indicates this happens with females. The women I talked with described one or two closest girlfriends who validated their values, attitudes, and experiences. The significant female friends supported their feeling of worthwhileness and their reality about males.

A final implication is that oral history proves to be a viable method for examining gender and communicative power. Rakow (1987) in her article "Looking to the Future: Five Questions for Gender Research," discusses the need for alternative methodologies for feminist scholarship. She states,

> Gender researchers must become more open to alternative methodologies if they are genuinely interested in feminist scholarship. The scientific and quantitative tradition that prevails in communication at the moment must be re-evaluated. A belief in "objectivity" and the goal of prediction and control of attitudes and behavior are not compatible with feminist research. While quantitative methods, if they are carefully scrutinized and the study carefully designed, can be of use to a feminist scholar, other methodologies are particularly useful in our studies of communication.
>
> If we are interested in recovering women's voices and experiences, styles and strategies, we might try in-depth interviewing, ethnography, life histories, and story telling. At the very least, we need to be sure we are studying real women in their real contexts....(p. 81)

In this study women told their stories rich in detail, that explained women's oral culture. Although the excerpts presented in this report might sound fragmented and sketchy, the humanness of what I was studying was evident in their entire life history narrations about their childhood, adolescence, and adulthood. The data was rich and the women's recollections sounded so real and believable that I could hear what their mothers told them, their girlfriends whispered to them, or they saw through their own eyes.

Oral history provided reliable data. I heard enough talk from the women to determine that inconsistencies were not present in their reports. The women appeared honest in the reminiscences. If I asked a question and they could not remember, they said so. If they remembered details, they reported them.

Schaef (1981, p. 28) talks about women's skills with recollection. Schaef states, "... most women develop an unbelievable capacity to remember details of events. If a couple has a quarrel, it is usually the woman who will remember what she said, what he said, the sequence of events, the setting, and how each seemed to be feeling at any point in the argument." As women told their narratives in this study, they reported incredible detail. Women reported dialogue, events, and feelings that happened as long as fifty years ago as though it had happened yesterday. It is impossible to determine whether their recollections are factual. But that's unimportant. The commonplaces women believe are based on their perceptions of what happened, rather than whether it did or did not happen.

This study was heuristic in design. Much of what it uncovers must be explored further. The findings indicate that women believe and act on commonplaces they learned about men and power. However, eight women's lives are not enough to generalize to a larger population of women. The disadvantage to quantitative studies is that the richness in data will be lost. The women's own stories, told through their own words, is what allowed the discovery of what and how women learn about relationships between men and women. The narrations, maxims, directives, gossip, conversations, and jokes of the eight women in their everyday expressions support Jordan and Kalcik's assertion (1985, p. xii) that women are in control of themselves and their worlds, and a sense of power is communicated by their folklore.

REFERENCES

DeCaro, F. (1983). *Women and Folklore.* Westport: Greenwood Press.

Dickson, P., and Goulden, J.C. (1983). *There are alligators in our sewers and other American credos.* New York: Delacorte Press.

Di Leonardo, M. (1987). The female world of cards and holidays: Women, families, and the work of kinship. *Signs: Journal of Women in Culture and Society* 12: 440-453.

Jordan, R.A., and Kalcik, S.J., eds. (1985). *Women's folklore: Women's culture.* Philadelphia: University of Pennsylvania Press.

Rakow, L. (1987). Looking to the future: Five questions for gender research. *Women's Studies in Communication* 10: 79-86.

Schaef, A.W. (1981). *Women's reality.* Minneapolis: Winston Press.

Spark, M. (1961). *The prime of Miss Jean Brodie*. New York: Dell Publishing.

Sullivan, H.S. (1953). *The interpersonal theory of psychiatry*. New York: W.W. Norton.

Webster, S. (1986). Women and folklore: Performing, characters, scholars. *Women's Studies International Forum* 9: 219-226.

Weigle, N. (1982). *Spiders and spinsters: Women and mythology*. Albuquerque: University of New Mexico Press.

Carole Spitzack

Re-Thinking the Relationship Between
Power, Expression, and Research Practices

Contemporary women are enmeshed in cultural conditions which demand a simultaneous prioritization and trivialization of the body. On the one hand, nonverbal studies show that physically attractive persons are perceived to be more competent, sociable, and intelligent than those who are unattractive;[1] on the other hand, women who make an effort to look attractive are thought to be insecure, tense, compliant before authority, and stereotyped in thinking (Aiken, 1963, 121). Closely linked to body stereotyping are ideological prescriptions which demand evidence for women's inequality. "Women who violate conventional sex role expectations," according to Pearson, "are often evaluated more negatively than are women who behave according to conventional sex role patterns" (1984, 216); yet, the everyday (perceived) concerns of traditional females, e.g., fashion, beauty, are presumed to be frivolous and not meritorious of serious questions, and already lend insight to scholarly conceptions of who and what is heard. I shall address the link between speaking privileges, gender, and power by discussing two issues: presentations of female vs. male experience and communication behavior; and the tendency to equate masculine behaviors with "normalcy" and feminine behaviors with deficiency (hence, in need of correction). Ideally, my discussion not only uncovers power strategies which exclude women while appearing to include them, but calls for a re-evaluation of the ideological underpinnings of our own notions of significance and scientific rigor in research practices.

From earliest socialization, as suggested by pink and blue infant color coding, it is imperative to use gender as a fundamental interpretive factor from which to perceive, evaluate, and judge behavior. The culturally sanctioned characteristics of males and females are frequently in opposition. The need to distinguish between males and females, notes Henley, "is felt with such urgency that it must be presumed to be preliminary to action. We intend to behave differently to people, depending on their sex" (1977, 93). Vetterling-Braggin, et al., observe that studies focused on gender differences generally find women to be "sympathetic, warm, soft-spoken, tender, gullible, childlike, loyal, and cheerful," while men are "self-reliant, independent, athletic, dominant, decisive, aggressive, and ambitious" (1977, 30). These divergent traits dictate a small, fragile, unintrusive

Carole Spitzack is Assistant Professor, Department of Communication, Tulane Unversity, New Orleans, LA 70118.

SYNOPSIS.....

Like several other authors in this collection, Carole Spitzack discusses the double bind that constrains women: they cannot simultaneously meet societal norms for success and womanliness. She contends that women's escape from this double bind will be through the expansion of our norms for success; this expansion would provide a variety rather than a dichotomy of choices for women.

Sptizack also echoes the call for expanded research methodologies. She points out the circularity and futility of trying to explore new topics and gain new insights with methods and mindsets that forecast and determine what insights will be found and how they will be interpreted. Moreover, she emphasizes that greater variety of methodologies does not mean an "anything goes approach to research." The goal of expanded variety in research methodology should be to explore greater possibilities, to look at what hasn't been observed before, and to look with truly open eyes.

appearance and manner for females and one which is large, strong, and commanding for males. Violations in sex role behavior typically signify deviant physical features as well. For example, homosexuals are envisioned as men who are weak, delicate, and passive, and lesbians are presumed to be large, abrasive, and aggressive women.

The traits aligned with masculinity are often associated, culturally, with greater health and normalcy than are those linked to femininity. Marilyn French (1985) argues that by the nineteenth century "it was generally believed that to be a woman was to be sick" (p. 358). Feminine sexuality formed the basis of this sickness, and imbued women's reproductive functions with pathology and deviance. The whole of female character is implicated by reducing women to sexual functioning, and "chaining" women to their bodies. Males, conversely, were not defined by reproductive activities. Maintaining greater distance between the body and the active ego, men are seen to rise above human biology and retain greater control over existence.

Nineteenth century conceptions of female pathology arose in conjunction with a socio-cultural prioritization of objectivist science. Science, as defined within androcentrism, produces two effects which further cement women's "illness." First, evidence for female malfunction is given validity through scientific experiment. Second, in verifying women's inability to dissociate from the body, traits which render women unsuitable for the practice of science -- subjective, emotional, unreasonable -- underscore women's inability to practice science. Concomitantly, masculine science and male traits become glorified, forming an opposition to the pathology of women.

Dichotomized male-female characterizations acquire particular significance for a study of power when it is realized that androcentric research practices glorify strength, individuality, and the capacity to control existence from a place outside the body. Along with control comes the ability to be objective and impartial, to avoid messy human connections which interfere with the acquisition of knowledge. Because these propensities are often presented as straightforward descriptions of reality, they appear to represent the experience of all cultural members. Consider the following examples from various topic areas in communication literature:

1) [T]he acquisition of communication competence is necessary to fulfill the general need of all humans to control their environment (Spitzberg and Cupach, 1984, 11).

2) The competent speaker has an appropriate measure of self-confidence and self-control. So central are self-confidence and control to effective public speaking that, in a sense, much of what we say in this book is aimed toward developing and strengthening this essential quality (Ehninger, et al., 1984, 19-20).

3) Focus your attention on ideas, not you and the other person. By confining your comments to the issue, you demonstrate your fairmindedness (Phillips and Wood, 1983, 74).

4) Higher status tends to result in greater personal power or ability to influence others. Increased power, in turn, tends to elevate an individual's status level. Power and status go hand in hand, reciprocally influencing each other (Tubbs, 1984, 154).

5) Competent researchers seek knowledge through careful and controlled inquiry. Those who allow biases and prejudices to confound their investigations come up with nothing more than distorted, slanted, or incorrect findings (Tucker, et al., 1981, 7).

These statements are not isolated cases, and not specifically endemic to communication studies. The logic of removedness is directly linked to what McIntosh describes as a "peaks and pinnacles" world view (1983, 4-5). Here, there are winners and losers, right and wrong, powerful and powerless distinctions:

> Both our public institutions and collective as well as inner-
> most psyches have taken on the hierarchical structure of
> this winning versus losing kind of paradigm. Those who
> climb up get power; we are taught that there is not power
> for the many but there is power at the top for those who can
> reach the peaks and pinnacles (5).

When placed next to traditional gender traits, females appear to lack the skills required for climbing, and are thus incapable of attaining power unless they can "overcome" socialized handicaps.

Numerous gender and feminist scholars have enabled a rethinking of female"deficiencies" by exposing the ideological underpinnings of masculine science. In particular, the presumed objectivity of science, aligned with masculinity, ignores and devalues women's communication strategies (Foss and Foss, 1983; Thorne, Kramarae, and Henley, 1983; Rakow, 1986; Spitzack and Carter, 1987). The very qualities that are seen to render female characteristics unsuitable for science are redefined to suggest that women and men operate through differing logics. Gilligan's critique of developmental perspectives in psychology, for example, displays that many research paradigms tacitly reflect dominant (i.e., male) biases, and consequently embrace a logic of separation and detachment (1982, 5-23). A logic of connectedness, which typifies feminine socialization, is absent and devalued. Lever's study of children's games provides a lucid example of these differing logics.[2] Here it is found that boys prioritize activity over relationships, while the opposite is true for girls. Conflict is likely to end a game involving female participants for it is more important to preserve relationships than to satisfy a predetermined desire to "win." Boys do not consciously decide to emphasize activity and/or winning, but rather are unaware of a contextual connection between relationships and activity. Conflict may erupt and relational battles fought, and all relationships are left intact. A "winning" logic suggests that personal relationships confound goal completion.

Conceptions of maturity and responsibility to others take opposing forms for men and women, In Gilligan's presentation of female discourse, "identity is defined in context of relationship and judged by a standard of responsibility and care" (160), male discourse reveals, "Relationships are often cast in the language of achievement, characterized by their success or failure" (154). In the former case, maturity is signified by a capacity to care and see oneself through relationships, while in the latter, maturity involves being able to establish distance between self and others, which may signify care through "fairmindedness." When the existence of an identity is contingent on involvement with others, "control" is a counter-productive, illusory notion. Separation from others, which is a necessary element in control, not only renders it impossible to interpret existence, but violates ethics of care and responsibility.

When research is clothed in neutral language, it is important to realize that neutrality itself, as Gilligan's studies show, embraces a particular ideological stance. Presentations of human experience incorporate and perpetuate dominant world views, and covertly exclude experience falling outside presumedly disinterested boundaries. Consistent with bi-polar logic which locates clear distinctions and categories, experience here is compartmentalized and reduced. Thus, when reading lists of gender traits as those presented above, or when confronting pornographic images of ourselves in film and advertising, it is apparent that the complexity of experiences has been omitted, yet it is difficult to argue with dominant truths presented as human truths. When a woman encounters peaks and pinnacles logic, her apparent choice is between control as defined by dominant culture, which promises payoffs, i.e., individuality, choice, strength; or impotence.

An effective critique of power requires a move beyond location of difference. Presenting two options where the only "reasonable" choice is to side with the powerful does little to dismantle prevailing domination strategies. Showalter's analysis of women's writing, and its relation to women's experience, does much to challenge dichotomized male-female identities (1981, 179-206). Female expression is often viewed as a "complex and perpetual negotiation taking place between women's culture and general culture" (199). Here, it is presumed that women, and men (whose interests enable them to define culture), exist in differing and conflicting experiential realms. The usefulness of these distinctions for advancing an understanding of women's experience becomes questionable, however, when women must live within masculine culture, defined and structured to exclude some and include others. Showalter proposed Ardener's model of the relationship between dominant and muted groups to suggest that women simultaneously inhabit two traditions:[3]

> Both muted and dominant groups generate beliefs or order-
> ing ideas of social reality at the unconscious level, but dom-

inant groups control the forms or structures in which consciousness can be articulated. Thus muted groups must
mediate their beliefs through allowable forms of dominant
structures. Another way of putting this would be to say that
all language is the language of dominant order, and women,
if they speak at all, must speak through it (200).

When examining women's experience, then, it is important to acknowledge
masculine-feminine differences, and to realize that reality and what is presumed
to be significant, are tied to women's expression. Categorical distinctions preserve the hidden interests of dominant culture while appearing to invite participation for those who conform to appropriate "human" standards. In reality,
female socialization permits a limited range of acceptable behaviors because a)
activities must meet role expectations, e.g., compliance, frailty, and b) behaviors
are judged by incorporating the very logic which discounts female experience.
Chelsler's study, *Women and Madness,* indicates that women are more apt to
display signs of abnormality in the (predominantly male) psychiatric profession:

> Men are generally allowed a greater range of "acceptable"
> behaviors than are women. It can be argued that psychiatric
> hospitalization or labeling relates to what society considers
> "unacceptable" behavior. Thus, since women are allowed
> fewer total behaviors and are more strictly confined to their
> role spheres than men are, women, more than men, will
> commit more behaviors that are seen as "ill" or "unaccept-
> able" (1973, 39).

Chelsler's observations contribute substantial insight to the power strategies of
dominant culture. If a woman displays traditionally female characteristics, e.g.,
compliance, interests in childbearing and family, she is more quickly deemed
"normal" than a woman who violated impartial definitions of normality; yet, it is
those very characteristics which retain subservient status.

In dominant culture, the aim is often detachment from the body, from
experience. Strong persons are able to rise above life circumstances, and are
thus able to govern and master the body. The problem for women is that a
substantial amount of cultural discourse centers on attention to the female body.
Women are encouraged to emphasize the body, to notice every ounce of added
flesh and every imperfection. The "body problem" for women is an insidious
demonstration of contemporary power tactics. Altering appearance for the sake
of social inclusion, in effect, demands removedness from the body and distance
from others. Speaking privileges are tied to physical exterior, which are different only in appearance from the desire to control existence through neutrality.
Rising above the body is needed for the creation of a socially approved exterior;
though one and/or for the production of impartial representations of experience

is often called narcissism and vanity, while the other is called rigor and validity. In this case, the seemingly opposing emphases are grounded in the sense-making apparatus of dominant culture through a complex manipulation of strategies which leaves all social members in assigned places.

It is arguable that interwoven variables merge to produce identities which, while claiming to offer clarity and participation, actually serve to dissect and constrain. In Banner's historical analysis of beauty in American culture, for example, it is noted that with every collective female expression of disfavorable circumstances, there has been a response which does not fundamentally improve everyday conditions for women, and may actually make matters worse by leaving underlying presumptions untouched. When suffrage movements voiced concern over the class oppression inforced by tight-lacing (since one required servants to aid in the accomplishment of an 18 inch waistline), the response was an assistance-free method of lacing (1983, 78-89). In principle, this "solution" is quite similar to pornographers' claims that female displays of nudity are an exercise of free expression for women.

Foucault's study of sexuality is particularly helpful in understanding contemporary power strategies which silence through an invitation to speak (1980). At the beginning of the 18th century, a regrouping of domination tactics occurred. The body became something in need of control by its inhabitant; something which, if left to its own desires, was capable of overtaking the individual. Confession, argues Foucault, was the means by which desires were transformed into discourse. Not coincidentally, this period was also marked by a surge of record keeping, as desires were articulated for purposes of freedom from body dangers, practices and thoughts entered the domain of public knowledge.

Confession for purposes of catharsis leading to self-knowledge is endemic to contemporary culture:

> The confession has spread its effects far and wide. It plays
> a part in justice, medicine, education, family relationships
> and love relationships; in the most ordinary affairs of every-
> day life, and in the most solemn rites; one confesses to one's
> crimes, one's sins, one's thoughts and desires, one's illnesses
> and troubles (Foucault, 1980, 59).

Foucault's observations are pertinent to the discrepancy between women's expression and dominant cultural demands, and the distortion of female experience. Women today are permitted to speak about their experience; to inform dominant culture of misconceptualizations, inequities,and unfair presumptions in an attempt to instantiate less homogenized, more favorable, identities. As Banner's study reveals, however, the "clarified" identity often not only fails to capture women's concerns, but induces further fragmentation and constraint. Foucault describes strategies which produce this effect:

> This form of power applies itself to immediate everyday life
> which categorizes the individual, marks him by his own

individuality, attaches him to his own identity, imposes a law
of truth on him which he must recognize and which others
have to recognize in him. It is a form of power which makes
individuals subjects . . . subject to someone else by control
and dependence, and tied to his own identity by a conscience
or self-knowledge (1982, 212).

Power, then, is not something wielded by some and denied to others, but is a
collection of complex and overlapping strategies which act directly and co-exten-
sively on bodies and speech. The illusion of dominant culture does not ultimately
rest in its pretense of global representation, but in its failure to notice the
materiality of power tactics which enjoy utopian status so long as individuals
embrace a logic of control.

If representations of women are juxtaposed to representations of men, female
experience is likely to appear deficient. If, however, alternative research strategies permit the critical capabilities of those who have not lost touch with the
body, others, and the world to become visible, a destruction of fragmented
identities can be accomplished. Developing such methods demands attention to
the dual citizenship of female cultural members, which in turn, requires that
accurate portrayals do not dichotomize and compartmentalize research findings.
I would argue that our concern not be centered on content only, but focus
simultaneously on the logic of women's thought. Moreover, presentations of
women's experience do more to dismantle oppressive prescriptions if those
prescriptions are found to be arbitrary and politically invested; a critique of
identity permits this kind of exposure and disruption.

These suggestions do not reflect an "anything goes" approach to research. To
read them in that light endorses dominant logic. Rather, I am arguing that
power strategies cannot be effectively questioned if methods and theories tacitly
perpetuate those power principles. My position encourages analyses which meet
women on their own ground, to present their lives and experiences in a manner
that does not instantiate defectiveness, requiring more confession of inadequacy,
and hence further trapping.[4] History displays the effortless co-optation of such
reductionistic presentations. If a goal of gender research is to unearth greater
possibilities for women, it is productive to display richness and variance through
systematic, rigorous, attentive analysis.

NOTES

[1] Malandro and Barker's discussion of the body as a component of communication behavior provides a review of such studies (1983, 31-49).

[2] My discussion of Lever's study is drawn from Gilligan's work (1982, 18-34).

[3] Ardener's model is presented by Showalter (1981, 198-200).

[4] I have elaborated both methodological and theoretical components of this position, as applied to female experience of cultural standards for appearance (Spitzack, 1985).

REFERENCES

Aiken, L. (1963). The relationship of dress to selected measures of personality in undergraduate women. *Journal of Social Psychology, 59,* 119-128.

Chernin, K. (1981). *The obsession: Reflections on the tyranny of slenderness.* New York: Harper-Colophon.

Chelsler, P. (1973). *Women and madness.* New York: Avon.

Ehninger, D., Gronbeck, B., & Monroe, A. (1984). *Principles of speech communication* (9th ed.). Glenview: Scott-Foresman.

Foss, K., and Foss, S. (1983). The status of research on women and communication. *Communication Quarterly, 31*(2), 195-204.

Foucault, M. (1980). In R. Hurley (Trans.) *The history of sexuality, vol. 1: An introduction.* New York: Vintage.

Foucault, M. (1982). The subject and power. In H. Dreyfus & P. Rabinow (appendix) *Michel Foucault: Beyond structuralism and hermeneutics,* pp. 212-224. Chicago: University of Chicago.

French, M. (1985). *Beyond power: Of women, men, and morals.* New York: Ballantine Books.

Gilligan, C. (1982). *In a different voice: Psychological theory and women's development.* Cambridge: Harvard University Press.

Henley, N. (1977). *Body politics: Power, sex, and nonverbal communication.* Englewood Cliffs: Prentice-Hall.

Malandro, L. & Barker, L. (1983). *Nonverbal communication.* Reading: Addison-Wesley.

McIntosh, P. (1983). *Interactive phases of curricular re-vision: A feminist perspective.* (Working Paper #124). Wellesley, MA 02181: Wellesley College, Center for Research on Women.

Pearson, J. C. (1985). *Gender and communication.* Dubuque: Wm. C. Brown.

Phillips, G. M., & Wood, J. T. (1983). *Communication and human relationships: The study of interpersonal communication.* New York: Macmillan.

Rakow, L. (1986). Rethinking gender research in communication. *Journal of Communication, 36*(4), 20-31.

Showalter, E. (1981). Feminist criticism in the wilderness. *Critical Inquiry,* 8 (2), 179-206.

Spitzack, C. and Carter, K. (1987). Women in communication studies: A typology for revision. I Quarterly Journal of Speech, 73(4), 401-423.

Spitzack, C. (1988). Body talk: Shaping women's bodies and women's expression. In A. Taylor and B. Bate (eds.), *Women communicating.* Norwood, NJ: Abbey Press, pp. 51-73.

Spitzberg, B. & Cupach, W. R. (1984). *Interpersonal communication competence.* Beverly Hills: Sage.

Thorne, B., Kramarae, C., and Henley, N. (1983). Opening a second decade of research. in B. Thorne, C. Kramarae, and N. Henley (eds.), *Language, gender and society.* Rowley, MA: Newbury House, pp. 7-24.

Tubbs, S. T. (1984). *A systems approach to small group interaction* (2nd ed.). Reading: Addison-Wesley.

Tucker, R. K., Weaver, R. L., & Berryman-Fink, C. (1981). *Research in speech communication.* Englewood Cliffs: Prentice-Hall.

SUMMARY AND CONCLUSIONS

Power is an easily understood concept, even though the definition of "power" varies somewhat from person to person. If we were asked to give a brief, yet comprehensive definition of power, we would say that one's power is the set of choices one has. The more choices, seemingly the more power. As Suzanne Condray's analytical case history of NOW's attempts to communicate shows, the limited power of NOW women was matched by their limited choices: they could not choose when they would be heard, they could not choose how they would present their message, and they could not choose what they would actually communicate.

In examining the relationship between communicative power and gender, many of the authors in this collection addressed the issue of choices. Several of the authors proposed that women's choices are limited or contradictory. Constance Staley, Barbara Crawford, and Carol Spitzack explored the double bind that women often face: women can choose an effective yet less acceptable communication style (a traditionally masculine style), or they can choose a less effective yet more acceptable style (a traditionally feminine style).

Even so, women need not and should not be constrained by this dichotomous choice. There are other options. Staley suggested that women side step this constraint and focus on skills and strategies. Other authors echoed this "side-step" approach. Valerie Endress explained that women need not accept traditional male definitions of power, definitions that limit women's (and indeed men's) choices, and thus limit their power. She proposed that we broaden our definitioin of power and at the same time broaden our conception of what constitutes effective rhetoric.

One frequent constraint on power is stereotyping. Stereotyping is a persistent limiter of power in that it narrows the choices of the person being stereeootyped: it narrows the choices of appropriate behavior, the choices of attainable goals, and the choices of how a person will be perceived by others. Stereotyping is responsible for the "double bind" described by Sayers and Staley, for the approximation (or lack of approximation) to the culturally determined "ideal" voice investigated by Valentine and Saint Damian, and for the interrelatedness of gender and politeness upon a person's perceived power which was explored by Hoar. In order to overcome these limitations of power, women must overcome stereotypes, both feminine and masculine. In order to avoid the constraint of the feminine stereotype, however, women need not conform to the masculine stereotype. Without the constraint of stereotypes, we are free to enlarge the scope of what is considered appropriate and effective, we are free to provide a greater number of options for "good" communication.

Finally, one of the stereotypes of research is the tightly controlled quantitative study. Like all stereotypes, it presents a narrow picture of what is really a complex endeavor, and it makes our scholarship less powerful because it narrows what we study and how we study it. To be sure, the tightly controlled quantitative study is a valuable tool, but it is not a tool for every research task. Several of the authors in this collection have suggested that feminist research -- indeed communication scholarship per se -- would be strengthened by the use of a broader range of methodologies. Indeed, the range of methodologies in this collection reflects this belief; for example, Sayers added an interpretive dimension to the quantitative approach and Romberger used the oral history to investigate the ways in which women learn about power in their relationships with men.

What is particularly interesting about the investigative techniques advocated and demonstrated in this collection is that they require interpersonal communication between scholars and the people they study, more interpersonal communication than is usually part of the process of tightly controlled quantitative studies. These expanded techniques underscore the value of effective interpersonal communication, these techniques put researchers in closer touch with the people they are studying, and they tap skills that many women have developed quite effectively.

In conclusion, when women's choices increase, so does their power. To be sure, we cannot have all the choices we might wish to have; but with a positive, creative approach, we can see choices that we did not see before, and we may even be able to create choices where none existed before. In short, we will be more communicatively powerful and we will be able to be ourselves.